Reconstructing Theory

Interpretations

This series provides clearly written and up-to-date introductions to recent theories and critical practices in the humanities and social sciences.

General Editor
Ken Ruthven (University of Melbourne)

Advisory Board
Tony Bennett (Griffith University)
Penny Boumelha (University of Adelaide)
John Frow (University of Queensland)
Sneja Gunew (University of Victoria, British Columbia)
Kevin Hart (Monash University)
Robert Hodge (University of Western Sydney)
Terry Threadgold (Monash University)

In preparation:
After a fashion, by Joanne Finkelstein
Hypertext, by Ilana Snyder
German feminist theory, by Silke Beinssen-Hesse
and Catherine Rigby

Reconstructing Theory

Gadamer, Habermas, Luhmann

Edited by David Roberts

MELBOURNE UNIVERSITY PRESS
1995

Melbourne University Press
PO Box 278, Carlton South, Victoria 3053, Australia

First published 1995

Designed by Mark Davis/text-art
Typeset by Melbourne University Press in 10.5/13 pt Garamond
Printed in Malaysia by SRM Production Services Sdn Bhd

ISSN 1039-6128

National Library of Australia Cataloguing-in-Publication entry

Reconstructing theory: Gadamer, Habermas, Luhmann
  Bibliography.
  Includes index.
  ISBN 0 522 84570 3.

  1. Gadamer, Hans-Georg, 1900– —Criticism and
  interpretation. 2. Habermas, Jürgen—Criticism and
  interpretation. 3. Luhmann, Niklas—Criticism and
  interpretation. 4. Hermeneutics. I. Roberts,
  David, 1937– . (Series: Interpretations).
121.68

Contents

Contents

Contributors

David Roberts is Professor of German at Monash University and is a Fellow of the Australian Academy of the Humanities. He is the author of *Art and Enlightenment* (1991) and co-editor of *The Idea of Europe* (1992) and *Europe in the 1990s* (1992). He is also, with Peter Beilharz and John Rundell, a co-editor of *Thesis Eleven*, the international journal of social theory.

Peter Beilharz is Reader in Sociology at La Trobe University. His most recent publications include *Labour's Utopias* (1992), *Transforming Labor* (1994) and *Postmodern Socialism* (1994). He is currently writing a book on the work of the influential art historian Bernard Smith.

Paul R. Harrison is Senior Lecturer and Convenor of Sociology at Queensland University of Technology. He is the author of *The Disenchantment of Reason* (1994).

John Rundell is Senior Lecturer in social theory at the Ashworth Centre for Social Theory at the University of Melbourne. He is the author of *The Origins of Modernity* (1987) and co-editor of *Between Totalitarianism and Postmodernity* (1992) and *Rethinking Imagination* (1994).

1

Introduction

David Roberts

The reception of German critical and social theory in the Anglo-American world has been overshadowed by the impact of French post-structuralism. The situation is not without irony, since Michel Foucault and Jacques Derrida are deeply indebted to German philosophy (Friedrich Nietzsche and Martin Heidegger), while Jürgen Habermas by contrast has been defending the legacy of the Enlightenment against French critics of modernity inspired by Nietzsche and Heidegger. This interest in the rational potential of modern society is the most significant dimension of the German contribution to contemporary social theory. It is represented most prominently by Habermas's reconstruction of the critical theory of the first generation of the Frankfurt School in the form of a theory of communicative action, and by Niklas Luhmann's reworking of the functionalist programme in sociology into a second-order cybernetic systems theory, universal in scope. Habermas and Luhmann have dominated German social theory since the end of the 1960s. For all their differences, evident in Luhmann's hostility to critical theory and in Habermas's critique of functionalism (the understanding of structures and processes in terms of their functions in the social system), they both represent a decisive break with what has been called the tragic consciousness of German social and cultural theory. Common to such diverse figures as Oswald Spengler, Max Weber, Georg Lukács, Martin Heidegger, Arnold Gehlen and Theodor Adorno, this tragic consciousness was clearly connected to the crisis and disintegration of the nineteenth-century liberal-bourgeois order under the shocks of World War I, the collapse of the Weimar Republic and the Nazi seizure of power. It was characterised by a deeply pessimistic reading of modernity. The processes of capitalist and bureaucratic rationalisation and the relentless technological domination of nature were seen as the destiny and fate of the modern world. There was no immediate reorientation of German social theory after 1945. A lengthy period of democratic 're-education', underpinned by West German economic recovery in the 1950s and 1960s, was required before a new generation could confront the lessons of German history and come to terms with the new realities of a 'westernised' society.

German sociology and philosophy after 1945 can be divided roughly into three groupings. First, a certain continuity with the Weimar period, represented most notably by Heidegger and Gehlen; second, the return from exile of such thinkers as Helmut Plessner, Max Horkheimer and Theodor Adorno, the founders of the Frankfurt School (among those who did not return from exile were Karl Mannheim, Norbert Elias and Herbert Marcuse); and third, the reception of American functionalism and empirical sociology. It was the reaction to this third component that led to the positivism debate at the beginning of the 1960s, initiated by Adorno's attack on American sociology (Adorno, 1976). The debate can be seen as a turning-point in sociological self-reflection in West Germany. It set Habermas on the path of reuniting critical and positive theory through the reception of American pragmatism, which distanced him increasingly from his mentors Horkheimer and Adorno. At the same time the rediscovery and enthusiastic reception of the writings of the Frankfurt School exiles—reinforced by the writings of Herbert Marcuse, the guru of the American New Left—played a key role in the student movement's challenge in the late 1960s to 'one-dimensional' society. Ironically, the outcome of this romantic challenge—a last 'revolutionary' expression of the radical critique of modernity, which called forth the charge of 'left fascism' from Habermas—was the recognition and acceptance of the western model of liberal-capitalist democracy. By the early 1970s West German society had come of age, and with Habermas and Luhmann post-war German social theory emerged in its own right. It is not by chance that Habermas is the first German theorist of democracy, nor that he and, more circumspectly, Luhmann align themselves with the tradition of Enlightenment thought against the pessimism of the German tradition, whose central sociological legacy is the theme of capitalist rationalisation and reification. This ambivalent legacy was taken up by Habermas and Luhmann in the wider context of an enquiry into the evolutionary rationality of the modern world, whose outcome has been the elaboration of comprehensive theories of society.

Habermas has transformed Max Weber's dualism of rationality and culture into the tension between system and life-world, which can be mediated only by recourse to the steering capacities of communicative reason. Luhmann by contrast cuts the link between social theory and normative values, replacing the 'old European' concept of political or civil society by the theory of society as a social system, whose determining characteristic is its differentiation into functional sub-systems. The elimination of questions of value, goals and needs from social theory is Luhmann's radical version of 'sociological enlightenment', which breaks with both conservative and critical theory's distrust of technology and science. His goal is the 'science of society', in which systems theory functions as the self-description of society in society, that is to say, as itself both result and expression of the evolutionary differentiation of society.

The order of presentation in the following chapters—Hans-Georg Gadamer, Habermas, Luhmann—is not to be understood as a progression, even if Gadamer's philosophical hermeneutics, which examines the connection between the theory and practice of interpretation and the understanding of the human condition, is concerned with our relation to tradition, whereas Luhmann seeks to integrate of the newest developments in cybernetics, biology and the cognitive sciences into his systems theory of society. Habermas occupies the central position because his dual conception of modern society—divided between the life-world (the source of the background assumptions of a shared culture) and system (the functional spheres of the economy and politics)—incorporates hermeneutics and systems theory at the same time as it relativises their claims. The relation between these three theoretical projects can be clarified by examining their treatment of language and meaning.

{Gadamer}

(a).-

The linguistic nature of our relation to other human beings and to the world is the central theme of Gadamer's philosophical hermeneutics (Gadamer, 1989). History and language form the encompassing frame which we cannot escape, and which we can experience only from the inside as the horizon of our experience. Together they comprise the tradition in which we are located, and which we appropriate and renew through our acts of understanding that connect the past with the present. Understanding is thus fundamental to all human activity, and is the means by which social life is realised. The power of tradition manifests itself in those 'pre-understandings' which guide interpretation. Since all knowledge and truth are historically based and linguistically mediated, the interpretation of texts of whatever kind involves a hermeneutic circle of understanding, whose outcome can never be the original meaning as such, but always meaning *for us*. Tradition is the ever-moving and changing fusion of the horizons of past and present. We can sum up Gadamer's key insight as follows: 'Language is the universal medium in which understanding is realised'. Understanding is an act of interpretation, and what interpretation accomplishes is a creative production rather than a reproduction of the text; that is to say, understanding is not an act of passive reception but involves an active application of the past to the interpreter's present.

In his 1966 'research report' *On the Logic of the Social Sciences*, published in 1970 (Habermas, 1988), Habermas seeks to determine the limits of a 'language-based interpretative' sociology, and in the process to clear the ground for his own enterprise, which he defines as a hermeneutically enlightened and historically directed functionalism. This theoretical programme—whose intention is interpretation, and whose interest is emancipatory—Habermas identifies as that of classical social theory from Marx to Weber. Habermas thus places himself in the grand tradition of social theory, whose ongoing task, he says, is to make the insights of functionalism serve the practical and moral self-constitution of society. It is this project of enlightenment that separates Habermas not only from Gadamer's emphasis on the authority of tradition but also from the functionalist logic of Luhmann. Habermas's hermeneutically enlightened functionalism is the starting point for his theory of communicative action. And here it is interesting to see how the basic elements of his theory emerge in his 1966 analysis of Gadamer's *Truth and Method*. Habermas agrees with Gadamer that the rational potential of language manifests itself in understanding. The capacity to learn our mother tongue gives us the capacity to learn other languages. The fact that we can translate from one language to another means that we are not enclosed in Ludwig Wittgenstein's monodological language games. We can assimilate the foreign and thereby extend our own horizon. Understanding and interpretation are realised externally by means of translation and internally through the socialising medium of language. In each case a fusion of horizons is involved, that is, the contextualisation of our own horizon within a larger whole. Like Gadamer, Habermas stresses the open and productive nature of the hermeneutic circle, which is endangered by the objectivism of scientific method because it breaks the relation between understanding and application. Gadamer explains this relation in terms of Aristotle's concept of practical knowledge, which is both reflexive in form (as a self-knowledge which contributes to the formation of the personality) and applicable to all dimensions of social life. Application provides the link to Habermas, since social life is constructed through communicative action. As Habermas puts it, hermeneutic understanding draws on the resources of tradition in order to clarify the possibility of action-oriented self-understanding and consensus among social groups, and as such it is an essential component of the social sciences.

For Habermas, however, there is both an internal and an external limit to Gadamer's hermeneutics. The hermeneutic contribution to social theory is limited internally by its failure to recognise the power of reflection inherent in understanding. The appropriation of tradition is not simply its continuing renewal but more importantly its rational testing and reconstruction. Even if pre-understanding—the authority of tradition—is the condition of understanding, reflection must seek to make the normative frame of understanding transparent. Language, however, is also the medium of the non-normative forces of domination and social power. Hermeneutics finds its external limit on the one hand in relation to ideology and on the other in relation to the objective institutional complexes of modern society, which can be tackled systematically only by a functionalist approach. The universal claims of cultural tradition must be relativised in relation to the objective dimensions of the economy and power. But equally the universal claims of function-alism must be relativised in relation to a shared cultural tradition.

At this stage, communicative action is conceived by Habermas in terms of an application which takes the form of collective learning processes, but there is a clear line of development from the rational potential of language to the theory of communicative action, which is assigned the task of holding the dangerously expansive logics of the economy and power in check. As against the economic–administrative system, the life-world consists of the set of pre-understandings which makes possible not only social life but also —beyond Gadamer—a reflexive relation to the transmission of cultural tradition, to the socialisation of individuals and the wider task of social integration. The life-world find its institutional extension in the public sphere, which provides the means by which social groups and society as a whole can develop a rational identity. Habermas thus works with a dualism of social integration and systemic integration, which are both the outcome of evolutionary processes. The rationalised life-world enables the differentiation of culture, society and personality; systemic rationalisation increases the self-regulating, steering capacities of society. This dualism cannot be reduced: the cultural reproduction of society excludes material reproduction, and functional systems ignore the identity of society.

The difference between Habermas and Luhmann can perhaps be best approached through the central place communication occupies in their respective theories. Communicative action for Habermas realises the rational potential of language; it is the process that constitutes consensus and identity. Luhmann denies that society can attain the rational ideal of identity, which he replaces by the factual difference between consensus and dissent. For Luhmann, society has neither reason nor subjects, individual or collective. Society is communication, or more exactly a communicative system. Language is not itself a system, but rather the medium of commu-nication and the structure that connects consciousness (psychic systems) and communication (social systems). It is not a system because the world is not divided by the one boundary between language and non-language, but by the many boundaries between systems and their environments. Communication accordingly takes the place of language in Luhmann's theory, and presupposes not only language but meaning; that is to say, meaning produces communication, and not the other way round. What is meaning? It is the ever present, taken-for-granted horizon of the world, and thus close to Habermas's concept of the life-world, as Luhmann acknowledges. Meaning and the world are coextensive, since the world forms the background presence (horizon) and reservoir of an inexhaustible potentiality of meaning that is actualised through selection (Luhmann, 1990). The world and meaning cannot be transcended or negated. There is only meaning in the world. The world thus signifies the unity of all the different systems and environments, and meaning in turn serves as the bridge between each system and its environment. In other words, the world is the correlate of meaning, and systems have access to the world through meaning. By 'systems' Luhmann means those self-organising, organic or psychic or social systems (cells, amoebas, immune systems, consciousness, communication, and so on) which draw a boundary between themselves and the world, and utilise this difference for their ongoing self-production ('autopoiesis'). All system-boundaries are meaning-boundaries, which reduce the complexity of the world through a selective openness to the environment. This preserves the system's identity and independence from the environment. The reduction of complexity is the condition of evolutionary differentiation, that is, the internal elaboration of complexity which embraces both natural and social evolution. In modern society, evolution has reached the point at which social differentiation has become autonomous. Politics, law, love, art, the economy, science, and so on have become autonomous and functionally differentiated communication systems, which are no longer organised according to Luhmann by reference to human beings as the subjects of communication. And this is the point at which systems theory emerges as the self-description of social evolution.

It is also the point at which we can grasp the architecture of Luhmann's theory. Habermas, as we have seen, combines life-world and system, a critically informed hermeneutics and a historically oriented functionalism (which has progressively incorporated Luhmann's systems-theoretical reworking and radical simplification of the functionalism of the American sociologist, Talcott Parsons). Luhmann combines the theory of society—the dimension of meaning—with the radical functionalism of his systems theory (Luhmann, 1987). This combination is enabled by the fact that the theory of society and systems theory both refer back to the problem of the extreme complexity of the world. As the system of all its sub-systems, society institutionalises not only the ultimate and most basic reductions of complexity, but also the ultimately attainable form of functional differentiation. Social evolution can thus be thought of as the process whereby the external complexity of the world is progressively replaced by ever more complex internal models of the reducible complexity of the world. That is why Luhmann has come to stress increasingly that systems are both observing and self-observing, and to formulate a constructivist theory of knowledge based not only on observation but also on the second-order observation of observation. For Luhmann, there is no way back from the reflexive second-order rationality of the functionally differentiated social system to the unity and identity of society. The decentring of society is the condition of differentiation. Or to put it in the theological terms Luhmann likes to employ: in the beginning was difference, not identity; and if we have lost God, we are left with the modern equivalent of the Devil—the observer, dedicated to sociological enlightenment.

Observers come into their own with the discovery of latency. Here Luhmann accords to art, and in particular the eighteenth-century novel, primacy in the observation of what others cannot see. The observation of the unobservable takes two forms: novel readers gain insight into the hidden and unconscious motives of the characters, but their attention is also drawn to the way the novel observes the world, to its (invisible) perspective or point of view. The novel is the modern genre *par excellence* because it adds second-order self-observation to first-order observation; for Luhmann this indicates that, in developing its own special form of observation, literature differentiates itself as a separate functional system of society. Another way of expressing this is to say that literature has become purely 'literature', that is, a self-reflexive observing system which views society from its own point of view, a distance made possible by print, which breaks the link between performance and reception. The reader's relation to the printed page is very different from that of the spectator at a dramatic performance. The literary (written and printed) text thus poses for Gadamer the test case for understanding, which is accomplished only when reading becomes a participating re-presentation that brings the written word back to life and presence.

The final chapter of this book examines the reception and application of hermeneutics, critical theory and systems theory to German literary theory since the end of the 1960s. The hermeneutic model is used by the Constance School of literary theory (Hans Robert Jauss, Wolfgang Iser) to explicate the act of reading and the nature of aesthetic experience. The critical theory of literature, associated with Peter and Christa Bürger, is close to Habermas's critique of hermeneutics, and shares also Habermas's distance from Adorno. Peter Bürger's guiding assumption is that aesthetic theory must reflect the historical development of art. Not only Adorno but the whole tradition of aesthetic theory since Hegel falls victim to the verdict of history. Bürger draws the conclusion that aesthetic theory must be transformed into a sociological investigation of the norms that govern the production and reception of literature. By the same token, hermeneutics must transform itself into an ideological critique of reception. The object of scrutiny is no longer the literary text, but what the Bürgers call the 'institution' of literature. Systems theory in turn places the literary institution within the literary system, and treats literature (and the other arts) as a social phenomenon which represents in its own way the evolutionary differentiation of society. This final chapter has a double purpose. The example of literary theory serves to indicate the applicability of social theory to one of the differentiated spheres of modern society. It also serves to remind us of the failure of contemporary social theory, not only in Germany, to combine in an adequate fashion social and cultural theory. But perhaps the contemporary separation of social from cultural theory is the price to be paid for breaking with the cultural pessimism of the classic figures of the German tradition from Georg Simmel and Weber to Adorno.

Gadamer and the Circles of Hermeneutics

John Rundell

It has now become a commonplace to say that 'we all interpret'. However, hermeneutics—the critical theory of interpretation—is the only current in western thought that has made this issue its own, notwithstanding its presence in both Marxism and that so-called science of phenomena, phenomenology. Through hermeneutics, interpretation has become part of our cultural self-understanding that only as historically and culturally located beings can we articulate ourselves in relation to others and the world in general.

The hermeneutic emphasis on interpretation emerged in the context of a culture which gave truth priority over interpretation in order to render interpretation problematic. The function of 'truth' was to control and authenticate interpretation. Hermeneutics reverses this regime by questioning the basis of truth, and by examining those interpretative contexts (often implicit or concealed) that give truth its meaning and its depth. In contemporary German social thought and philosophy Hans-Georg Gadamer has been the predominant figure, whose principal publication, *Truth and Method*, I will examine later. This work has done more than any other in contemporary hermeneutics to place interpretation—as well as the ways in which 'interpretation' itself has been interpreted—at the centre of the way we view human activity.

This chapter is divided into two sections. The first establishes the central themes and preoccupations of hermeneutics. Using phenomenology as an initial point of contact and contrast, it outlines the hermeneutic tradition and especially its indebtedness to the Enlightenment and Romanticism, both of which left hermeneutics with unresolvable conceptual difficulties. The second section considers the ways in which these conceptual difficulties have been tackled (first by Martin Heidegger and more recently by Gadamer) in attempts to foreground the primacy of interpretative contexts and activity.

Themes, issues and historical background

In the wake of Kantian transcendentalism and Hegelian philosophy of the spirit, twentieth-century German philosophy has been propelled by two forces in addition to critical Marxism and neo-Romanticism: phenomenology and hermeneutics. This has occurred also in the historical and social sciences, including social theory, which the Germans link with philosophy under the title of the human sciences (*Geisteswissenschaften*). Each has set itself against positivism, which has marked not only the German intellectual landscape but also the topography of western thought generally (Giddens, 1984; Frisby, 1976; Bubner, 1981; Schnädelbach, 1984; Habermas, 1988).

The main concept which phenomenology develops is that of the 'life-world'. This refers to the everyday knowledge we take for granted: those practices and orientations that form and remain the unexplained basis of scientific investigations. It emerges in Edmund Husserl's later philosophy, and is developed in a sociological register in the work of Alfred Schutz and Thomas Luckman.

Hermeneutics is also interested in illuminating the everyday life-world of social actors and scientific and philosophical investigators. Its main concern is not with phenomenological conscious-ness as such, but with those dimensions of understanding and interpretation that are required in everyday life, philosophical enquiry or scientific investigation. In this sense, hermeneutics focuses on the meaning of what is said, read and heard. A central preoccupation of hermeneutics is therefore with language, and in particular with texts. Unlike phenomenology, it is not only interested in the life-world context here and now, but also questions this contemporaneity from the perspective of those historical contexts that condition it. In other words, everyday life, philosophical investigations and scientific enquiries are shaped inevitably by our understandings and interpretations of the past.

In this way, the investigative context in which phenomenology operates is maintained also for hermeneutics, but with a difference. Sociological phenomenology usually concentrates on the minutiae of relations between social actors, and how such interaction is established and maintained both linguistically and non-linguistically. For hermeneutics, the implicit assumption is that communication and thus understanding are intrinsically difficult and problematic. In other words, social actors or interlocutors experience a permanent 'gap' in comprehension. The intersubjective contexts expand to include those between speakers both present and absent; that is, between texts and readers, the present and the past. Hermeneutics deals, especially in its modern form, with the transmission of culture, and particularly western culture. This culture has two peculiarities: it is predominantly a written rather than oral culture, and its origins coincide with the birth not only of philosophy (the Greek Enlightenment between the fifth and fourth centuries BC) but also of the Jewish and subsequently Christian traditions. Moreover, because it is a written culture, cultural transmission through the written word (texts) raises a double-sided problem. One is the issue of the authenticity of the texts, especially since these often survive only as fragments and incomplete manuscripts: in order to deal with this problem, the historical specificity of the text in question has to be gauged. The other issue is the question of authorial authenticity, that is, whether a text ascribed to a particular author (for example, Plato or Aristotle) is genuine. This double-sided problem cannot be approached by treating such documents as objects on to which archaeological techniques can be superimposed, because historical time always intercedes between the present and the past. In the absence of an objective correspondence between present and past, an interpretative effort is required in order to bridge these gaps in comprehension. Because no singular and unitary meaning emerges from any speech act or text, the fluidity (and thus multiplicity) of meaning is the starting point for hermeneutic analysis.

Moreover, hermeneutics should not be regarded simply as a method for transmitting culture in the form of a historical knowledge which might solve problems of authenticity and truthfulness. It is also a theory of reflexivity in a double sense. Hermeneutics assumes that historical knowledge becomes conscious of its own processes of self-formation, usually by recognising that this knowledge itself has a historical context. This is what Giddens (1984) terms a double hermeneutic. However, such recognition leads to a deeper sense of reflection. Historical consciousness is viewed as the path to self-consciousness or historically formed self-knowledge. Called *historicity*, in the Heideggerian sense, it refers ultimately to the issue of identity. A historically informed reflective consciousness shifts the idea of identity from the taken-for-granted present, and attempts to throw it into relief by opening it up to the power of the past. The question emerges, then, as to how past and present relate to one another, and thus on what basis and on what terms cultural identity develops and continues. Consequently, issues of continuity, critique and change are also at the heart of hermeneutics.

Because it is concerned with the problems of meaning, intersubjectivity and reflexivity, hermeneutics has a longer history than phenomenology. Originating in Greek antiquity, the word alludes to the god Hermes, the wing-footed bringer of messages (Palmer, 1969; Ermath, 1981; Mueller-Vollmer, 1986a; Dilthey, 1990; Ormiston and Schrift, 1990a; Bruns, 1992). As Palmer notes, 'Hermes is associated with the function of transmitting what is beyond human understanding into a form that human intelligence can grasp', thus making intelligible that which otherwise is unintelligible (Palmer, 1969:13). Etymologically, the word stems from the Greek verb *herméneuein* and the noun *herméneia*. These are usually translated respectively as 'to interpret' and 'interpretation'.

Between the etymology of the word and its classical usages, three different dimensions of hermeneutics emerged. They focused on either the expressive or explanatory qualities of the text, as well as on the issue of its adequate translation. Each considers and constructs the issues of meaning, intersubjectivity and reflexivity in different ways.

The issue of adequate translation can be discussed first because it throws into relief aspects of the other two. Hermes and the priests may be considered the first hermeneuts because they mediated between two worlds, making what was initially foreign into something that could be understood. The activity of translation renders visible something which remains unnoticed and taken for granted in everyday language use, namely that there are barriers between worlds (where 'worlds' refers to cultures, perspectives and persons) which make understanding problematic. In this sense we are all translators, attempting to understand and interpret others who appear in varying degrees foreign to us. Moreover, the activity of 'translation' also directs our attention to the centrality of language in this process. As Palmer again points out, '"translation" makes us aware of the fact that language itself contains an over-arching interpretation of the world . . . Language is clearly a repository of cultural experience, we exist in it and through this medium; we see through its eyes' (Palmer, 1969:27). Translation, then, disturbs or disrupts meaning as a matter of course (and in an act of violation and violence, some post-structuralists would say), as the translator searches for appropriate words, metaphors and phrases to render one language intelligibly into another. It thus calls for sensitivity, or what one might call *hermeneutic engagement*.

The activity of translation directs our attention to the two other dimensions of hermeneutics—the performative and the explanatory. In antiquity messages were often delivered orally. The expressive demeanour of the messenger or translator (priest or warrior) was often an important component of the message, just as it is in the rhetorical style of political speech-making in order to win votes and convince enemies. Here, performance is as much part of the hermeneutic exercise as understanding is. In this context, writing was viewed by some (and famously by Plato in his dialogue *Phaedrus*) as a loss of expressive power, a self-estrangement from speaking.

The message, however, must be not only announced but also explained. Here a close relation is forged between translation and understanding. Explanation involves understanding the content of a message in the process of its translation, as well as seeking to establish its truth or falsity. To establish the authenticity of text and author requires cognitive or intellectual rather than expressive or engaged efforts, and assumes a capacity for reason and rational articulation.

Explanation remains central to modern and contemporary hermeneutics and philosophy. By 'modern' I mean the culture of modernity from the thirteenth century to the present, and more specifically the ongoing dispute between Enlightenment and Romanticism. Explanation raises the problem as to whether there is a method for arriving at truth. Does truth already presuppose an interpretative context, constituted by preformed points of reference and prejudice which already predispose a particular search *for* a particular truth *to* a particular truth, and which ensure that this search is undertaken in a particular way? This context (and those preformed points of reference) is termed *the hermeneutical circle*. As the first form of reflexivity referred to above, it encompasses all explanation: consequently, the explanation even of objective contexts such as 'nature' has an interpretative dimension (Palmer, 1969:20–7). As Gadamer insists, the hermeneutical circle is our universal human context (Gadamer, 1977).

In many respects, modern and contemporary hermeneutics still live in the shadows of these formulations. The problems of expressiveness, explanation and translation still provide a rich legacy to modern and contemporary hermeneutics, which ought not be seen, however, as merely a continuation or series of replays of this aspect of ancient Greek thought. One reason is that, historically and conceptually, these three dimensions of hermeneutics tended to develop in their own (although not unconnected) ways, and to become specialised techniques of cultural transmission, particularly with respect to the continuity and identity of the west. From late antiquity to the Christian Middle Ages rules developed for interpreting sacred texts, and which included the rabbinical approach as well as those of the Greek tradition. Hermeneutics also evolved into a method for interpreting Roman jurisprudence during the Renaissance. Hermeneutics thus developed in specialised areas, particularly theology and jurisprudence, in order to define a heritage viewed as continuous, or to retrieve and redefine those aspects of it which had been suppressed or lost.

Two important cultural innovations have decisively shaped the identity of the west and the forms of modern hermeneutics. One is the cultural creation of Protestantism, and the problems that its rupture from Roman Catholicism generated for religious and scriptural interpretation. Catholic Christianity had emphasised tradition and authority as the basis for establishing the true meaning of holy text, and reaffirmed this at the Council of Trent in 1546. Protestantism, notwithstanding its own dogmatic preferences, opened up the possibility of a plurality of interpretations.

Protestant hermeneutics broke with the tradition of revelation mediated by 'the voice', in which ultimate authority was deemed to be vocal, not textual. Writing was only a trace of vocal authority, which resided largely in the personal representative of God (the prophet or the priest). During the Protestantisation of scriptural interpretation, however, the idea of unquestionable authority receded. Textual truth and authenticity were to be established not by the unquestioned authority of a Church empowered to distinguish orthodox from heretical meanings, but by the self-sufficiency of the text (Feher, 1991). This gave authority to both text *and* interpreter. Protestantism thus adds a new tension to those inherited from pagan antiquity, which had receded during the formation of the Christian world view and its theological doctrines. On the one hand, if interpretation resides in the text, an appropriate method must be found for excavating it, because interpretation is still assumed to be related to truth. On the other hand, a plurality of interpreters and interpretations becomes possible, all unconstrained by fears of heresy, and all potentially autonomous and authentic (Mueller-Vollmer, 1986a:2; Bruns, 1992:139–58).

The second cultural innovation, for which Protestantism is also a background, is the Enlightenment, especially the German transcendental philosophy established by Immanuel Kant, and the Romantic responses to it. Hermeneutics here emerges in its modern form. Its modernisation involves a double transformation of the meaning of 'understanding', as well as the introduction of the idea of the creative subject. One outcome is a series of problematic separations between 'explanation', 'expressiveness' and 'translatability'. This occurs in the context of an ongoing commitment to explanation, which the Enlightenment transposes into the question of understanding.

The key figure here is Kant, even though he is usually seen as standing outside the hermeneutical tradition. In his *Critique of Pure Reason* (1781) Kant reformulates the notion of understanding (and hence of explanation) on transcendental grounds. For Kant, understanding is a capacity (or what he terms a 'faculty') present in all human beings, which enables experiences to be brought together under rules which are given names as concepts. We understand something because we can explain it through conceptual articulation, and we can conceptualise because of an unknown (and unknowable) capacity for reasoning. This concern with understanding involves a double strategy: interpretation is subordinated to the integrating activity of understanding, and the development of an enquiry into the proper conditions for understanding. Modern hermeneutics during this period tended to emphasise the issue of 'proper conditions', and became increasingly preoccupied with two of them: history and philosophical anthropology, that is, with an image of the human as an expressive being who has language.

In the Kantian formulation, the possible conditions for understanding and explanation belong to the universal capacity of reason, which exists beyond time and space. Hegel argued in his *Phenomenology of Spirit* (1807) against this transcendental formulation, and posited that reason can be understood only historically, because it is teleological—it has a purpose, an end. Modern hermeneutics criticises both transcendental and teleological notions of reason and history. The hermeneutical task is to historicise reason. This *historicisation of understanding*, as Schnädelbach terms it, 'treats not only universal reason as a basis of understanding, but also the original production of meaning and the process of historical transmission as part of the newly understood historical process and teaches that all factors should be seen . . . as something historical' (Schnädelbach, 1984:112). This historicisation of understanding thus bridges the distance between the present and the past. It does so, however, not in a correspondent or determinate way (which constructs an 'objective' historical truth from an assumed array of empirical 'facts'), but rather in a manner which enables the interpreter or hermeneut always to enter into new historical relations with the past. This makes historical knowledge not only fluid but also never complete. As Schleiermacher notes, historical interpretation, or an understanding which understands itself historically, 'is an endless task' (Schleiermacher, 1977:41). History is thus not a limit to knowledge but a condition for it.

The other condition is language. History and language are inseparable, for it is only through language 'that all understanding is historically mediated' (Wachterhauser, 1986:9). More than this, though, it points to the specific characteristic of the human species, and also the particular means through which relations are constituted between its members as well as with the world in general. Language points to the active and formative dimension of the human species. It is the necessary 'vehicle' through which humanity objectifies itself and develops its capacity for reflection and culture. Language, then, both realises and gives form to the human capacity for consciousness; it is not a referent or representative of objects. Following Charles Taylor, this emphasis on language can be called 'the expressivist turn' of German thought at the end of the eighteenth century as it began to settle its account with the rationalist current of the Enlightenment. Initiated by Johann Herder, that 'turn' was continued by others such as Wilhelm von Humboldt. The search for the linguistic conditions of understanding is related, although not reducible, to another formative influence on modern hermeneutics, namely Romanticism. Romanticism shapes hermeneutics in two particularly modern ways: partly through its emphasis on the new idea of the creative artist and the creative imagination (which Romanticism makes its own), and partly through the formation of a cultural universe which emphasised emotions and affects rather than a cognitively centred rationality.

Within this double context of the historicisation of understanding and the linguistification of the human subject, hermeneutics was to develop in two different although not inseparable directions. *Romantic hermeneutics* emphasised expressiveness and translatability under the aegis of the creative subject: Schleiermacher is the representative figure here. In the other formation, known as *reflective hermeneutics*, methodological principles appropriate for the study of history were emphasised, particularly in the work of Wilhelm Dilthey, whose unfinished and thus never published *Critique of Historical Reason* was to provide the epistemological principles or method through which a historical knowledge of humanity and society could be attained. Methodological issues were not the only cornerstones of modern hermeneutic analysis, which has engaged with two other major problems. One is the idea of direct access to authorial intent, which often comes at the expense of broader historical understanding; the other is the development of dialogic models which emphasise intersubjectivity. Both Romantic and epistemological hermeneutics (as they developed under the shadow of Kant) can be viewed as paradigms of understanding construed as *mutual sociability*, which also implies a reflection on how our cultural identity is formed. These models encountered, however, three crucial problems. One was epistemological: how could the idea of an objective method for the human sciences (Dilthey) be sustained except at the cost of intersubjectivity itself? Another was metaphysical: the category of life, which underpinned both romantic and epistemological hermeneutics, concealed the basis for which hermeneutic reflection could emerge. The third was ethical: the intersubjective relations posited in hermeneutics implied *norms* of intersubjectivity which could not be explicated either in part (Schleiermacher) or fully (Dilthey).

It took a revolution in hermeneutics to break this impasse. That revolution occurred in two stages. The first thinker to redefine the hermeneutical problem is Martin Heidegger, who proceeds in the wake of Friedrich Nietzsche's hammer-blows against philosophy, and attempts to locate hermeneutics beyond and outside metaphysics. *Ontological hermeneutics* emerges when the hermeneutical problem is rethought in the context of the problem of being. While continuing to concern itself with the problem of cultural transmission, ontological hermeneutics subsumes and subordinates it to the question of being, namely what 'being' might be. The focus then becomes the nature of language. Gadamer continues this transformation in contemporary German philosophy. By reconnecting hermeneutics with an ethics of sociability (intersubjectivity), he takes hermeneutics beyond the specific problem of the human sciences in order to explore more deeply the issue of human existence.

Ontological hermeneutics

Heidegger's recasting of the hermeneutical circle

Heidegger is not usually regarded as someone who 'belongs' to the hermeneutical current in German thought. He is often seen instead as a philosopher who reformulates the hermeneutic problem from within his own philosophy. Nevertheless, he should be located there for two reasons: first because he provides a constant source and inspiration for Gadamer's own ontological hermeneutics, and secondly because he is self-consciously a hermeneut in the way he uses texts to speak across and about time (history). Consequently he gives to the notions of understanding and interpretation an ontological and deeper sense than is evident in previous formulations, including those by Kant and Dilthey.

Heidegger's revolution in philosophy (including hermeneutics) is first announced in *Being and Time* (published in 1927), and continues in such later works as 'The Origin of the Work of Art' (written in 1936), 'Letter on Humanism' (written in 1947), and 'What is Called Thinking' (written in 1954). All of these works are continuing reflections on the ontological condition of being, and as such are simultaneously reflections on language. Gadamer is influenced by Heidegger's work in both these periods.

In *Being and Time* Heidegger's task is to critique the conditions which lie behind scientific and categorical thinking: this type of thinking, he argues, has preoccupied, framed and 'built' western philosophy since the Greeks developed it. In order to achieve this task, he has to reposition the notions of interpretation and understanding. Understanding becomes the more primordial (Heidegger, 1985:2–35, 169–224; Mueller-Vollmer, 1986a:32–7; Connolly and Keutner, 1988; DiCenso, 1990).

Heidegger radicalises Dilthey's hermeneutics, and disconnects it from nineteenth-century occupations with scientificity. He does this by forsaking any claims to an objectivity and a truth outside hermeneutics, a move Dilthey was unable to make. Hermeneutics is no longer merely a method in Heidegger's hands, but becomes instead the condition for a reflection on how humankind relates to being. Heidegger argues that the ontological dimension of understanding has remained concealed because of the way in which language has been conceptualised as expression and grammar. In one aspect it is a 'developed way of conceiving' (Heidegger, 1985:199), in which an object or entity that is part of our experience is framed into something 'about which' we can know. The moment an entity is transformed and presented as an object, knowledge of it can be discovered only by seeing it as a disconnected 'thing' constituted by certain properties. This, for Heidegger, is the kind of technical thinking that results in an unfettered mastery over and manipulation of nature. According to Heidegger, the concealment of ontology began when the Greeks (and especially Plato and Aristotle) constructed the *logos* (inner rationality) as the means for discovering something through its properties. He terms this thinking, in which technical 'understanding' is verbalised through judgements (correct/incorrect, true/untrue), 'apophantic' (Heidegger, 1985:195–203, 55–63), because it is 'un' (*àpo*) 'showing' (*phantes*).

Heidegger argues that this type of thinking is already an interpretation or 'disclosure' of the world. Statements or assertions about entities or objects already signify or *point out* lived relational contexts through an array of meanings, which by their very presence predispose and anchor things in the world (Heidegger, 1985:195–203). In order to demonstrate this, Heidegger begins with an enquiry into the hermeneutics of human existence which is simultaneously an enquiry into its ontology. This shifts the meaning of hermeneutics away from Dilthey's formulation (which is a mutual and reflective understanding reached through common lived experiences) towards the primacy of the nature of understanding itself.

Some brief remarks need to be made at this point about Heidegger's ontological project. In his view, human existence is inherently concerned with Being, which takes ontological priority over the question of beings. However, he argues that conventional ontologies internal to western thought have approached the question of Being (*Sein*) from the side of beings, entities or those things which simply 'are' (*Seiendes*). In other words, Heidegger argues that conventional ontologies conflated the question of Being with that of beings. In Heidegger's view, one should begin again to rethink the question of Being, which also entails a positive re-evaluation of Greek philosophy before Socrates, and to separate Being from beings. The first step along the way both to separate Being from beings and to clarify the ontology of Being is to investigate the status of the enquirer. In other words, in *Being and Time*, the question of ontology should be approached initially from the side of the enquirer's being-in-the-world which includes the 'impurities' of everyday thinking, as well as historical consciousness.

The term he uses for being-in-the-world is *Dasein* (Heidegger, 1985:27).

This move in Heidegger's argument has a double effect. First, this initial step ensures that there is neither a congruence nor a coming together of being-in-the-world and Being: rather they are close, yet distant. For Heidegger, Being's simultaneous closeness to and distance from being-in-the-world can be disclosed and initially 'bridged' (although never completely) only in the exposition of being-in-the-world. Thus not only is understanding always a disclosure across a gap, but the gap itself is experienced as a void between being-in-the-world and its unknowable 'other', Being.

Second, this separation gives greater weight to the hermeneutic dimension than in other previous formulations. It makes the capacity for understanding central to being-in-the-world and prevents it from being subordinate and subject to a specialised technique, such as exegesis. In Heidegger's view, an understanding can never be achieved which is not already embedded or immersed in a condition of prior understanding. Heidegger accepts Kant's version of understanding as a transcendental condition, that is, as something which occurs prior to knowledge but of which we cannot *know* anything. At the same time he argues that understanding is knowable because there are always prior understandings of the world. This makes understanding not so much cognitive as experienced and historical. He gives this his own ontological twist. For Heidegger, 'understanding is that mode through which the possibilities and potentialities of his life are disclosed to a person' (Mueller-Vollmer, 1986b:84).

This disclosure takes place through a pre-existent series of understandings which already predetermine a stance towards, and an understanding of, objects, tools, institutions, purposes, and so on. Although we can never get to know these things as entities, according to Heidegger we experience them as a doubleness: for that understanding of contexts which allows a thing to be understood has simultaneously a history prior to one's own individual understanding. We are thrown into our world, and this world is a hermeneutical circle. For Heidegger, however, it is not a vicious circle of misconception and deceit, but a circle of appearance which conceals and belies a truth.

If we see this circle as a vicious one and look for ways of avoiding it, even if we just 'sense' it as inevitable imperfection, then the act of understanding has been misunderstood from the ground up . . . what is decisive is not to get out of the circle but to come into it the right way. This circle of understanding is . . . the expression of the existential fore-structure of Dasein itself . . . [in it] is hidden a positive possibility of the most primordial kind of knowing. (Heidegger, 1985:194–5).

In *Being and Time* this type of understanding, as an ontological condition, is different and separable from interpretation. To interpret, according to Heidegger, means to cultivate, select and target an aspect at which we consciously aim. This we are able to do by what Heidegger terms 'fore-sight'. Interpretation is formulated already in pre-existent concepts which are taken in the first instance 'as natural' by the interpreter: interpretation is grounded in a fore-conception or set of presuppositions which are already 'there'. As Mueller-Vollmer comments, 'interpretation originates in under-standing and is always derived from it . . . [It] is nothing but the explication of what has already been understood' (Mueller-Vollmer, 1986a:35).

Although language is not the starting point in *Being and Time* for a rethinking of the hermeneutical problem, it none the less attains a privileged status in Heidegger's thought because of its closeness to ontological thinking. Heidegger interprets language as both 'discourse' and 'signification'. Discourse opens on to the intersubjective nature of being-in-the-world. This makes disclosure a shared activity with others, in which a communication involves not only speaking but also hearing, listening and keeping silent. In each of these aspects of communication (and they are not really separable), understanding is presupposed as an ontological herme-neutic which 'is constitutive for the Being of the "there"' (Heidegger, 1985:208). Moreover, this emphasis on a shared ontological understanding also presupposes, at least in *Being and Time*, a co-presence of interlocutors, such that understanding emerges from neither one side nor the other, but is given in the fore-structure of understanding itself, which is 'prior' to the speakers. What is required is not a hermeneutic *effort* but a hermeneutic *acceptance*. As we shall see, this aspect of Heidegger's discussion of language in *Being and Time* is significant for Gadamer's own version of ontological hermeneutics.

This ontology of understanding also frames Heidegger's critique of language as 'signification', that is, a system which signifies, assigns and forms through grammatical rules and principles. Heidegger argues against those grammatical and empirical (now termed 'analytic') views of language in which there is 'a staunch belief in the dogma of unequivocality, of semantic identity' (Frank, 1989:215). He is especially unconvinced that meaning can be derived from the grammar of language, which is fundamentally apophantic. In *Being and Time*, however, Heidegger cannot spell out what language is; all he can do is reaffirm its ontological condition as discourse in the way described above. To describe what language is becomes Heidegger's task in his later works. This is not undertaken from the vantage point of an ontological hermeneutic, but by elucidating the gap between Being and being-in-the-world. As he says in *Being and Time*, but in a way which almost anticipates this later work, 'the doctrine of signification is rooted in the ontology of Dasein. Whether it prospers or decays depends on the fate of this ontology' (Heidegger, 1985:209).

In order to further his project of recasting ontology, Heidegger increasingly investigates the nature of Being itself. As Bubner remarks, 'Heidegger's "Letter on Humanism" of 1947 [which marks the later period] is an attempt to surpass himself philosophically' (Bubner, 1981:47). Heidegger's ontological emphasis on the pre-understanding of the world—which both shapes and provides a stronger ground for relations between humans, as well as between the non-human and the human—is transposed to an emphasis on how Being reveals itself to humans. In order to avoid the conventional trap of ontology (which posits the idea of pure revelation), Heidegger argues that Being both reveals and conceals itself. Both aspects are primordial. 'Unhiddenness' is not simply a dimension of things or beings as they are correctly known: it is originary. Likewise, hiddenness or concealment should not be viewed as error or untruth, because it also is originary. As Heidegger recasts his ontology, language now becomes the place in which the ontological conflict between concealment and revelation occurs.

No longer viewed as discourse or signification, it is a poetic expressiveness which exists prior to the damage done to it when shaped by metaphysicians like Plato and Aristotle. Language thus becomes 'the house of Being, owned and pervaded by Being' and as such 'is the clearing-and-concealing advent of Being itself' (Heidegger, 1973:156).

Heidegger further attempts to avoid the conventional ontological trap of pure revelation by adding not so much an active human dimension (for this features in other ontologies, such as Hegel's), but rather one which is not structured apophantically. Being is there to be revealed by humans in their (inadequate) thinking of it. For Heidegger, the representative 'thinkers' are poets and philosophers, because they can escape the trap of thinking categorically. Humans (as poets and philosophers) come close to Being only by residing in its house as guardians, who establish an ecstatic and poetic rather than a cold and technical relation with Being. Only in this poetic manner can one enter that clearing of Being that represents the realm (the void between being-in-the-world) in which there is simultaneously disclosure as well as concealment. This later development in Heidegger's thought, however, takes us quite a distance away from his earlier work as well as from traditional concerns with hermeneutics. The result is a conceptual tension in his work between, on the one hand, an ontological expansion which gives primacy to understanding and interpretation and, on the other hand, a view that this historical embodiment is a movement away from an original truthfulness or insight about Being itself.

Gadamer's task is not to unite these divergent tendencies in Heidegger's work but rather to draw on them for his own purposes. He aims to restore the reflective moment to hermeneutic consciousness, without recourse either to a set of methodological principles which require external objective standards or to the subjectivism of Schleiermacher.

Past and present revisited: Gadamer's critical ontology of hermeneutical reflection

Gadamer's recasting of the hermeneutical problem culminates in his *magnum opus, Truth and Method*. After settling his accounts with previous hermeneutic traditions, he presents his own pro-gramme in the second half of the book. This book is principally a work of critical reconstruction from a hermeneutic standpoint. In many respects Gadamer's work is as much an argument with Schleiermacher and Dilthey as a dialogue with Heidegger. This makes it a reflective and therefore critical reconstruction of the historicity of western thinking since Heidegger. It is thus also an argument against a contemporary culture that still identifies scientific knowledge and its practices with progress and truth, and assumes that such knowledge gives epistemological legitimacy to all forms of knowledge, notwithstanding the critiques of scientific culture. As such, Gadamer's work can be aligned broadly with current critical thinking which includes such diversities as the Frankfurt School of social theory, Jürgen Habermas, Michel Foucault's critiques of the scientific *episteme*, Richard Rorty's anti-foundational pragmatism, and deconstructionism (Gadamer, 1981; Bernstein, 1982, 1985). Instead of dwelling on this aspect of Gadamer's work, however, I will concentrate on his development of ontological hermeneutics.

In Gadamer's view Schleiermacher's attempt to recreate the original condition for authorial creativity—and thus 'to understand the text at first as well as then even better than its author' (Schleiermacher, 1977:112)—is 'a futile undertaking' (Gadamer, 1989:167). For Schleiermacher, interpretation emerges not from the interpreter but the author, and is revealed in terms of what Schleiermacher calls 'style'. This refers to 'an author's distinctive way of treating the subject [and] is manifested by his organisation of his material and by his use of language' (Schleiermacher, 1977:149). One must learn the author's style of writing and be sensitive to its nuances in order to detect as much what it doesn't say as what it does. By means of such hermeneutical sensitivity, which Schleiermacher calls 'the divinatory method', the interpreter is transformed 'into the author [and] seeks to gain an immediate comprehension of the author as an individual' (ibid.:150). In order to underpin this method, Schleiermacher draws on the category of 'life', transposing it from the metaphysics of nature into the category of empathy. 'Life' means the 'lived experience' and thus creative activity of the author. It is through this act of empathy that the gap between creator and interpreter is assumed to be bridged.

In the end, according to Gadamer, this 'divinatory method' is unworkable because it is anchored ultimately in an idea of alienation. 'Reconstructing the original circumstances, like all restoration, is a futile undertaking in view of the historicality of our being', Gadamer argues from the vantage point of his Heideggerianism; for what is reconstructed, a life brought back from the lost past, is not the original. What is handed on is only 'dead meaning' (Gadamer, 1989:167). Furthermore, behind this idea of alienation, according to Gadamer, is Schleiermacher's particular attitude to texts and thus cultural transmission. 'His hermeneutics . . . had in mind texts whose *authority* was undisputed . . . The interest that motivated Schleiermacher's methodological abstraction was not that of the historian but the theologian . . . [His] goal was the exact under-standing of particular texts' (ibid.:197). In other words, the idea of unquestioned authority not only aligns creativity with the author and not the interpreter, but also locates authority in the past. In both cases the monologue of authority blocks off dialogues with the present.

Dilthey, with equally 'problematic consequences' (according to Gadamer) was 'always attempting to legitimate the knowledge of what was historically conditioned as an achievement of objective science . . .' (ibid.:231). This attempt to make historical knowledge reflexive was the explicit aim of Dilthey's hermeneutics. Yet, for Dilthey, hermeneutic reflection must concern itself with methodo-logical principles, which in the end remain objective in character. Dilthey's efforts to construct (or at least convey) a hermeneutical circle which is both open and indeterminate are undercut by his reliance on a concealed Cartesianism. For notwithstanding his critique of the methods of the natural sciences, Dilthey 'remains entangled in the ideal of objectivity championed by the . . . historical school against which [he] levelled so much criticism' (Palmer, 1969:178). He borrows from the sciences the concept of inductive method, and then links it to a concealed Cartesianism, a set of methodological principles with which Descartes hoped to immu-nise knowledge from tradition, prejudice and opinion. In order to claim objectivity, Dilthey must assume a standpoint *outside* the historically fashioned hermeneutical circle, and from which he can-not remain reflexively open enough to doubt his own assumptions and question his points of departure. This standpoint outside the hermeneutic circle is for Dilthey *life*. As Gadamer notes *'for Dilthey the connection between life and knowledge is an original datum'* on which to ground the claim for objectivity (Gadamer, 1989:236, original emphasis). Palmer points out that this type of reflective method 'is incapable of revealing new truth; it only renders explicit the kind of truth already implicit in the method . . . In the method the inquiring subject leads and controls and manipulates . . . [in order to] bring the object under his grasp' (Palmer, 1969:165). Yet this central category of *life*—which lifts experience and thus knowledge above both historical individuals and cultural forms—has implicit metaphysical dimensions with respect to its own self-movement and developing self-consciousness. As Gadamer notes, Dilthey's notion of 'historical consciousness' (the historicisation of understanding) simply replaces Hegel's 'teleological reason' (a reason with a purpose and an end). Moreover, and equally importantly, both Hegel and Kant regarded reason as the basis for a human capacity to reflect on freedom. But for Dilthey, 'life' has replaced freedom as the value or horizon to which reflection refers for its orientation. This is why in Dilthey's hands the implied value of critique, which is internal to any project of hermeneutic reflection, comes to a standstill. Dilthey's notion of 'life' cannot deal with those same ethical issues and questions which emerge from a hermeneutics of reflection, such as, 'Who am I?' 'In what way might I live?' 'How might I live with others?' 'What are the values, the points of orientation'—what Gadamer will term 'horizons'—'which enable me to so live?'

Two issues, which are no longer methodological, emerge from Gadamer's arguments with Schleiermacher and Dilthey. One concerns the intersubjective dimension of hermeneutics, which makes its normative dimension explicit; the other relates to Gadamer's regrounding of hermeneutics within ontology. For Gadamer, both Dilthey and Schleiermacher obviate and collapse both the distinction and the relation between past and present: Schleiermacher collapses the present into the past, whereas Dilthey makes the past contemporary with the present. However, for Gadamer, this intersubjective relation exists (like all others) in tension, and is not outside a normative frame of intersubjective reference. As he says somewhat programatically, 'the hermeneutic task consists in not covering up this tension by attempting a naive assimilation of the two but in consciously bringing it out' (Gadamer, 1989:306). This idea of what might be termed *intersubjectivity in tension* becomes one side of Gadamer's reformulation of hermeneutics. Constructed as a relation of question and answer between interlocutors, it is through this dialectic that Gadamer attempts to re-establish that dimension of reflexivity which, he argues, has been blocked by previous hermeneutic programmes. The other way in which Gadamer reformulates hermeneutics is to rework Heidegger's ontology. This elevates historicity (historical reflexivity) to the position of a universal condition through Heidegger's disclosure of the fore-structure of understanding, and views language as the condition through which such elevation takes place. Together, the forestructure of understanding and language constitute the human condition. They thus establish the universality of hermeneutics, because (for Gadamer) 'being hermeneutic' means not only being-in-relation with another, but also and simultaneously being-in-language.

In his essay on 'The Universality of the Hermeneutical Problem' Gadamer begins from a common observation: that misunderstanding is as common as understanding. In Gadamer's view, one difficulty with Schleiermacher's hermeneutics was that it aimed at avoiding misunderstanding. The taken-for-granted starting-point of hermeneutic analysis for Gadamer, on the other hand, is that misunderstanding occurs by virtue of being in relation to others (that is, in the relation between I and Thou). The distance which defines this relation has been interpreted variously as alienation, a loss of authentic meaning, or a move towards and away from true understanding. In conventional hermeneutics from Schleiermacher to Dilthey, 'misunderstanding' is thus viewed as an untruth which has to be controlled methodologically.

Explicitly following both the Heidegger of *Being and Time* and the late Heidegger who views untruth as primordial, Gadamer argues that there is neither a chasm nor an experience of alienation in the relationship between I and Thou. Instead, 'there is always a world already interpreted, already organised in its basic relations' (Gadamer, 1977:15), a hermeneutical circle of primordial understanding which is also historical. Strangeness and alienation are merely relative features; they indicate a movement away from the 'home' of understanding, and towards possible enrichment on the basis of what has already been understood. In this way, and in an argument against subjectivism, Gadamer claims that any attempt to base historical reflection or a move into unknown territory on an individual life or an individual text is bound to fail, because it makes history and historical reflexivity a private and singular affair:

> history does not belong to us; we belong to it. Long before we understand ourselves through the process of self-examination, we understand ourselves in a self-evident way in the family, society and state in which we live. The focus of subjectivity is a distorting mirror. The self-awareness of the individual is only a flickering in the closed circuits of historical life. (Gadamer, 1989:276)

Gadamer's critique is two-pronged. Hermeneutic reflection is embedded in and begins with the primordiality of understanding, that 'fore-structure' (following Heidegger) into which we are thrown, and through which we disclose a world. Gadamer's term for this idea of fore-structure is 'prejudice' which predetermines the nature of perspectives and judgements about the world. The capacity to make what appear to be personal judgements and choices is at best a second-order phenomenon. Prejudices (that is, pre-judgements) rather than judgements 'constitute the historical reality of being' (ibid.:277). Gadamer's notion of prejudice becomes an extension of the Heideggerian notion of falsity or primordial untruth (ibid.:270; DiCenso, 1990:96–102). At this level of ontology, hermeneutics clarifies the conditions in which understanding takes place. Because it is neither a procedure nor a method, the interpreter cannot separate 'productive' prejudices (which lead to understanding) from the 'unproductive' (which result in misunderstanding). Rather, as Gadamer notes, 'this separation must take place in the process of understanding itself' (Gadamer, 1989:296).

Gadamer's notion of prejudice becomes the basis for his critique of the Enlightenment. In one of his most interesting arguments, Gadamer contends that the Enlightenment's confidence in reason developed in the context of a modernity which wanted to separate itself from a tradition which legitimated judgements so that it (the Enlightenment) could make judgements on the basis of its own internal criteria. The Enlightenment was to furnish the categories of judgement from reason, without recourse to a prior history or meaning. In severing its own relation to the tradition out of which it emerged, the Enlightenment jettisoned the idea of tradition altogether. For Gadamer, the problem with the Enlightenment is that it lives entirely in and is obsessed with the present (ibid.:271–7). Gadamer states that the fundamental prejudice of the Enlightenment is 'the prejudice against prejudice itself' (ibid.:270).

As a result of the Enlightenment's version of reason and its transposition into the historicisation of understanding, the temporal distance between past and present was either ignored or collapsed. Gadamer's notion of prejudice serves both to resuscitate this idea of distance and to restore it from collapse by locating it as an ontological condition. This is achieved by reintroducing a positive notion of tradition. Following Heidegger in *Being and Time*, Gadamer views time (history) as something which does not need to be bridged. It is itself 'the supportive ground of the course of events in which the present is rooted' (ibid.:297), and Gadamer terms this tradition. The hermeneutical circle, then, is a combination of prejudice (or fore-understanding) and tradition. As one commentator puts it, 'Gadamer's point is that the contemporary inquirer *needs* the pre-judgements embodied in traditions in order to develop a historically-based dialogical enquiry' (DiCenso, 1990:100).

This combination, accordingly, is the ontological starting point for that hermeneutic consciousness and reflection which generally has been termed understanding. For Gadamer, understanding emerges neither from rational judgements (in the Kantian sense) nor from 'the closed subjectivism' of Romanticism and Romantic hermeneutics. It emerges instead out of the tension produced by the temporal distance between past and present, and which is expressed in terms of the relation between Thou and I. The movement of recognition in Hegel's master–slave dialectic (explicated in his *Phenomenology of Spirit*) becomes the starting point for Gadamer's own theory of hermeneutic reflection. Hegel's dialectic refers to the capacity for reflection which is based on the mutual co-presence and potentially reciprocal recognition between an I and a Thou. It is thus grounded in a self-referential hermeneutic circle. Reflection operates, for Hegel, through the development of increasingly higher levels of understanding which are themselves the work of Reason. While Hegelian hermeneutics are in this sense developmental, they are none the less closed. Gadamer departs from this version of dialectical reflection, although taking with him Hegel's emphasis on the interactive or dialogic dimension of hermeneutics. He wants to establish a hermeneutics, which, while acknowledging the condition of being inside a hermeneutic circle, is a form of reflection that holds this circle open.

Gadamer thus argues initially that 'hermeneutics must start from the position that a person seeking to understand something has a bond to the subject matter that comes into language through [tradition]' (Gadamer, 1989:295). However, this is neither a continuous nor self-evident tradition, nor is it one of unquestioned agreement. It is a product of hermeneutic *work* rather than of either sensitivity (Schleiermacher) or acceptance (Heidegger), and it is based on the polarity of familiarity and strangeness. While prejudice is an ontological *precondition*, tradition is an ontological *outcome* which also involves the work of reflection. Reflection emerges in the play between what is both familiar and strange to us. Understanding is thus a reflexive second-order activity: it emerges in that interplay between tradition and interpretation which enables the hermeneutic circle to be opened up. And crucially, for Gadamer, this opening-up is initiated by a question. Gadamer calls this type of reflection 'historically effected consciousness' and it is at the centre of his hermeneutics (ibid.: 300–2).

For Gadamer, the opening of the hermeneutic circle is effected not only by dialogue (and specifically Plato's Socratic dialogues) but also the mode of questioning through which dialogue is not only initiated but constituted. To raise questions is in Gadamer's view a creative and productive act, which initiates a dialogue between present and past, although on the basis of a problem in the present. Interpretation always begins with a question which challenges the completeness of the hermeneutic circle. As he states, 'the real power of hermeneutical consciousness is our ability to see what is questionable' (Gadamer, 1977:13). 'It opens up possibilities

and keeps them open' (Gadamer, 1989:299). In Gadamer's hermeneutic ontology, questioning is part of the exposition of Being; it is
a ruptural and fissuring process. Furthermore, Gadamer insists that
the principle of openness keeps the dialogue going between
interlocutors. In 'the process of question and answer, giving and
taking, talking at cross purposes and seeing each other's point'
(ibid.:368), the communication of meaning occurs. When this
dialogic form takes place across time, textuality is brought into the
living present as a conversation between interlocutors who are
thereby mutually present.

However, for Gadamer, this is not a one-way process, for it is
not only the present that asks questions. By means of texts,
fragments and traces, the past also asks questions to which we in
the present must be open. But we can be open to them only if we
go beyond the historical horizon they present us, that is, by
incorporating our own comprehension into their meaning. In other
words, unlike Schleiermacher, Gadamer is adamant that present
understanding is built into the understanding of texts from the
past.

This 'fusion of horizons' is the central aspect of Gadamerian
hermeneutics. To ask a question is neither to interrogate a void nor
to assert merely one's own point of view. Rather, we ask questions
from within our own horizon of understanding, which is itself
limited by interpretative biases. Gadamer invokes the notion of
'horizon' to convey this; it is 'the range of vision that includes
everything that can be seen from a particular vantage point'
(ibid.:302). This range enables one to move from a singular horizon
of the present to a broader historical one, and by so doing
simultaneously confront both one's self as 'other' and the other
(the past) as a 'self'. In this way the present is challenged by the
past. Once consciously developed, dialogues with the past (or
traditions) can uncover biases at both ends. The 'space' and activity
of this encounter are for Gadamer a 'fusion of horizons', which is
the phrase he uses to describe his own version of a reflective
hermeneutics in tension. In that fusion, both present and past
disclose themselves in a hermeneutical act which is always not
only communicative but ongoing. This gives Gadamer's central
notion of tradition a fluidity which some critics (such as Habermas,

1990a) have denied. But as DiCenso remarks, 'every time the tension of the text as "other" is experienced, the horizon of the inquirer undergoes a transformation to accommodate new insight' (DiCenso, 1990:102). This makes the nature of the hermeneutic enterprise radically incomplete. Because questions are initiated from the present, others can always be asked. They will act not merely as a check against closure, but also to initiate further openings, insights and transformations.

If the 'space' and activity of hermeneutic reflection constitute 'the fusion of horizons', this is because cultural universes can be conveyed only by language. As Gadamer states, *'the fusion of horizons that takes place in the understanding is actually the achievement of language'* (Gadamer, 1989:378, original emphasis). Gadamer can argue this only if a further ontological project lies behind his already ontologised hermeneutics, which relies on the Heideggerian transformation of understanding. This time, though, Gadamer draws not on *Being and Time* but rather on the later Heidegger to develop his hermeneutics. The paradigm of an *inter-subjectivity in tension* (and thus reflection) must be supplemented by an ontology not of the understanding but of language itself.

For Gadamer, the world does not become an object of language, constructed, as it were, outside us. Following Heidegger, 'language' is not a means of thinking in terms of statements and factualness; instead, 'the object of knowledge and statements is always already enclosed within the horizon of language' (ibid.:450). It is a question not merely of enclosure, but of the status of language as ontology: 'the being that can be understood is [itself] language' (ibid.:474). This means not only that 'our verbal experience of the world is prior to everything that is recognised and addressed as existing' (ibid.:450), but also (and at a deeper level still) that this world is built up in language. This remains the case, in Gadamer's view, despite the scientific levelling of language to a technical sign-system which invades our everyday experiences and linguistic practices. Language, as ontology, persists whenever dialogue begins; it is a space inhabited by lovers, who are often in the in-between-of-language (Gadamer, 1977).

More expressively and in the spirit of the later Heidegger, Gadamer insists that the ontology of language is denoted by the paradigm of poetry which is the most primordial dimension of Being. Poetry stands for a speculative creativity that produces new meaning. Hermeneutically, this is the process through which new questions worthy of being answered emerge, and which require language (as poetics) to keep the circle open (Gadamer, 1989:470–1, 575). At a deeper level still, language is the totality that surrounds and holds us, even prior to consciousness (Gadamer, 1977:41). In this way, it absorbs the work of the imagination, and of hearing and listening, and ensures that language is 'continually on the way to language' (Gadamer, ibid.:228).

Each aspect of Gadamer's hermeneutics—intersubjectivity and ontology—can become a point of reference for his friendly or interested critics (cf. Shapiro and Sica, 1984; Silverman and Ihde, 1985; Frank, 1989; Michelfelder and Palmer, 1989; Habermas, 1990a, b, c; Ormiston and Schrift, 1990a). There are at least two points of contact by contemporary philosophy and social theory with Gadamerian hermeneutics—the Habermasian and the Derridean. The more recent interest by deconstructionists in Gadamer's work stems from their common roots in, especially, the later Heideggerian ontology, with one marked difference. While Gadamer emphasises presence and co-presence, Derrida emphasises absence or the other side of Being which he terms *différance*. However, in the context of Gadamer's own German hermeneutic context, his earlier dispute with Habermas introduces many of the issues with which contemporary philosophy and social theory are still preoccupied. Leaving to one side the issue of ontology, we now turn briefly to the Gadamer–Habermas dispute.

Habermas's 1970 critique of *Truth and Method* rests on a communicatively grounded paradigm of intersubjectivity. He takes as his starting point the image of sociality which is built into Gadamer's project (that is, what 'form of life' it promises, and what its utopian horizon might be). This is particularly important at a time when 'the horizon of modernity is shifting' (Habermas, 1992:3–10) and the certainty of critical perspectives can no longer be assured. Our point of departure, however, is Habermas's more recent remarks on Gadamer in his 1983 essay entitled 'Reconstruction and Interpretation in the Human Sciences' (Habermas, 1990c).

Habermas acknowledges Gadamer's role in what has come to be known as the 'interpretive turn' (Rabinow and Sullivan, 1979) which is now accepted as the underlying principle in social sciences. The interpreter's participant role in giving meaning to an already given cultural product can no longer be denied. Gadamerian hermeneutics in particular 'avoids the embarrassment of a language analysis that cannot justify its own language game' (Habermas, 1990a:222). As hermeneuts we are already in the circle of the language game. In this way, too, interpretation becomes problematic not because of misunderstandings caused by something new or unfamiliar; on the contrary, interpretation is situated 'in thoroughly mundane encounters' (Habermas, 1990b:42). But because this circle is open in ways portrayed so convincingly by Gadamer, the unfamiliar can be brought into context and thereby into dialogue. This should produce not only an extension and fusion of horizons, but also (as both Habermas and Gadamer insist) agreement (Habermas, 1990c:25–6, Gadamer, 1990:273).

For both Habermas and Gadamer, agreement is reached through a fusion of horizons. Notwithstanding Gadamer's unfortunate terminology, this fusion of horizons does not result in a one-sided assimilation of the 'other' to 'us'. Rather, according to Habermas, 'it must mean a convergence . . . of "our" perspective and "their" perspective—no matter whether "they" or "we" or both sides have to reformulate established practices of justification' (Habermas, 1992:138). Moreover, for both Habermas and Gadamer, this fusion of horizons (produced by interpretative acts) is achieved by a critical thinking that raises questions and doubts about society. Beyond the immediate concerns of social science, Gadamer's ontological hermeneutics is in this respect as much a practical and critical philosophy as Habermas's theory of communicative action. Gadamer's hermeneutics is first and foremost a philosophy of praxis: it carries within it the interpreter's relation to the idea of the social good, which itself is carried forward by tradition. Hermeneutics, in Gadamer's view, thus keeps traditions alive. Moreover, and crucially for Gadamer, through it tradition becomes the anchor and consequently point of authority to which interpretation refers.

Habermas and Gadamer dispute this critical point. In Habermas's view, Gadamer undermines hermeneutics' claim to reflection by his commitment to the idea of tradition: he turns his own insight into the structure of pre-judgement against reflection itself, that is, 'into a rehabilitation of prejudice' (Habermas, 1990a:236). Even though Gadamer invokes the idea of 'prudence' inherited from the Greek and particularly Aristotelian notion of *phronesis* (in which the goods of a society are learnt and critically judged within the limits of good sense), 'the methodic cultivation of prudence' shifts the balance towards authority and away from reflection. As Habermas baldly states: 'Gadamer's prejudice for the rights of prejudice certified by tradition denies the power of reflection' (ibid.:237).

This is the case whenever there is continuity of culture, and 'authority is detached from insight and blindly [asserts] itself' (ibid.:236). Here, reflection gives way to the facticity or factualness of tradition. It becomes even more problematic when continuity is in doubt or has been fissured. For then there is neither recourse to the richness of tradition (as Gadamer is inclined to view it) nor anything 'beyond' tradition to which reflection could refer, except the ontological priority of language itself. And here, for Habermas, ontological hermeneutics reaches its limit point: 'it remains incomplete as long as it does not include a reflection upon the limits of hermeneutic understanding' (Habermas, 1990b:253). But this critique of Gadamer largely misses the mark. What is at issue is whether an Aristotelian philosophy of praxis can be revived to address the limits of a technological civilisation (as Gadamer and MacIntyre believe), or whether (as Habermas and Richard Rorty think) we need a praxis philosophy which does not draw on the traditions of antiquity (Kelly, 1990:70–89).

Gadamer responds to Habermas's criticisms by asserting the self-limitation of the hermeneutic enterprise. Rather than being a criterion of truth, hermeneutic reflection (according to Gadamer's own self-understanding of *Truth and Method*) is 'limited to opening up opportunities for knowledge which would otherwise remain unperceived' (Gadamer, 1990:284). In this sense, the criticism of his recourse to tradition is based on a misunderstanding. Habermas, according to Gadamer, equates the dialogical opening-up of tradition with its naive, pre-reflective application. As Gadamer says, 'tradition exists only in constantly becoming other than it is' (ibid.:288).

In Gadamer's view, hermeneutics is more modest than the claims of a critical theory which stands in the wake of Marxism. It can offer only a partial perspective as it dissolves blockages to knowledge by confronting one prejudice with (admittedly) another. In this respect (and notwithstanding his own statements), Gadamer's hermeneutics culminates not in a theory of understanding as 'agreement', but in an implicit theory of *interpretations which must stand to differ* (ibid.:289). What results is a model of contemporary society which could be termed *open-ended indeterminacy*. Interpretation is our permanent condition, for the tensions it gives rise to can never be overcome or (in the Hegelian sense) transcended. Hermeneutic reflection makes us confront our finitude, and therefore the limits to what we think we can control (Gadamer, 1981:150).

3

Critical Theory— Jürgen Habermas

Peter Beilharz

Critical Theory and Jürgen Habermas—the tradition identified with the Frankfurt School, and its leading contemporary advocate. Simply to state these two names is to suggest some of the complexities and issues involved in making sense of the Critical Theory tradition. Let us take each term in turn. *Critical Theory*, today, is understood by transatlantic intellectuals to refer to the concerns of both philosophy and literary theory. For criticism, of course, is a widely shared practice, neither peculiar to Germany nor a monopoly of the left. After Jacques Derrida and deconstruction, after Jean Baudrillard and cultural studies, 'critical theory' is widely practised in its lower-case form, and associated generically with the interdisciplinary conduct of critique. Why then *critique*? To speak of 'critical' theory is to make it plain that other kinds of theory are less than fully or properly critical. And this was, indeed, Max Horkheimer's intention in distinguishing between 'traditional' and 'critical' theory. The founding Director of the Frankfurt School, Horkheimer was committed to the principle of Marxism, championed in our own time by Jürgen Habermas, that theory ought have a practical intention. Both thinkers also set out from the premise that, contrary to the Marxism of Karl Marx or Georg Lukács, the proletariat had now lost its historic moment; to change the world was an interesting demand, but a less than straightforward proposition. By the 1930s the working class looked more like part of the problem than its solution. The working class, in this view, had been integrated.

Whatever 'critical theory' is taken to refer to today, the connotations of German Critical Theory here are evident. In this particular context, Critical Theory refers to the project of the Frankfurt School, so-called for its place of origin in the Institute for Social Research in 1923. Yet the signifier 'Frankfurt' itself is only partly suggestive of what Critical Theory was to become after some of its Jewish leaders (such as Theodor Adorno and Horkheimer) fled Nazism to take refuge in (of all places) California, home of the Hollywood Dream. Not that these thinkers—Adorno, Horkheimer, and variously Herbert Marcuse, Erich Fromm, Leo Löwenthal, Otto Kirchheimer, Franz Neumann and Friedrich Pollock—all shared the same purpose. They had different capacities and interests, enthusiasms and limits. In this founding generation Adorno was to remain the towering presence. Only Marcuse in the radical years of the 1960s achieved a similar degree of influence, close perhaps to that in recent times of Michel Foucault.

Critical Theory, in this context, might be briefly defined therefore as the German School (or better, circle) of cultural critique identified with Frankfurt neo-Marxism. Enter Habermas, our second constituent term, and the subject of this chapter. Habermas is the leading intellectual representative of second-generation Critical Theory. Born in 1929, he was among other things Adorno's assistant during the period when the School returned to Germany after World War II. The relationship between the two generations is a complicated matter, for to skim through work by, say, Adorno and Habermas is to wonder what connection there might be at all. Adorno was a philosopher and the author of an argument often aligned with cultural pessimism, the logic of which is that the twentieth century and even modernity itself are long arcs of irrevocable decline. This was a philosophy of history—most powerfully evident in *Dialectic of Enlightenment*, written still during the war but published in 1947 (Horkheimer and Adorno, 1973)—cast in the shadow of the Holocaust. It inverted Marx's and Lukács's sense of a triumphal onward march wherein the proletariat would establish socialism upon the pre-existing cultural achievements of the bourgeoisie. After Auschwitz, the direction of history was downward, the dream of enlightenment could no longer be sustained.

While Habermas's work does not return to a Lukácsian optimism, a sense of qualified historical progress nevertheless marks his work. This sense finds its culmination in the argument that modernity is an unfulfilled project, less a tangent of irreversible decline than a moment of perpetual stalling within a field of greater possibilities (Habermas, 1981). But this is only part of the difference between first-generation and second-generation Critical Theory. Readers of Adorno and Habermas who scan more widely cannot help but be struck also by the differing extent of their claims. Adorno's philosophical mode, elevated into an art form, cultivates the aphorism (Adorno, 1974). What is both striking and difficult about Habermas's work is that, rather than being cryptic or evocative, it becomes expansive and systematic to the point almost of being encyclopaedic. In this regard, the project of Habermas is more like that of the syncretic Cambridge sociologist Anthony Giddens. For Habermas's work is characterised by an ever-expanding optic, culminating in the most comprehensive of his works, the two-volume *Theory of Communicative Action*. While the meaning of Critical Theory is transformed across the generations, the extent of Habermas's own work also changes dramatically. Its early scope may be defined as the reconstruction of Marxism as a critical theory, and more specifically as a critical sociology. This is a significant peculiarity in Habermas's reworking of Marxism or critical theory, for sociology in Germany had in the meantime been effectively destroyed by Nazism. To reconstruct sociology after the war meant also at least partly to Americanise it. Thus Habermas's key thinkers shift from Marx and Freud to Talcott Parsons, Jean Piaget, Lawrence Kohlberg, and so on.

All this hints at the problem of reception. For Habermas's work shifts historically, sometimes engaged more with the arguments of the first generation, and at other times less so. But it is also received by different readers in different ways. Several issues immediately suggest themselves here. The first is that since the 1980s Habermas has been received or presented especially as the advocate of modernity against postmodernism. The dominant image of Habermas into the 1980s is the Voice of Reason, a Teutonic opponent of Foucault and Lyotard. This indicates the immediate problem, namely that his work is frequently read out of context. And this is a major issue, for Habermas's own method of reading and interpretation presumes that there is a larger logic or trajectory at work in any thinker, a whole of which the fragments are parts. The second issue is that the English-language presentation of Habermas focuses on his big theoretical books, and has hardly engaged with his more directly political interventions against, for instance, revisionist attempts to rewrite or to erase the history of the Holocaust, or against racism in the new, reunited Germany (e.g. Habermas, 1989b). Habermas has a political and oppositional stature that rarely breaks through in English, except perhaps when the few desperate remaining revolutionary Marxists appropriated his work after 1989, or when theologians turn to it for inspiration—for Habermas remains a philosopher of hope, however residually (Callinicos, 1989; Peukert, 1989; Holub, 1991; Dews, 1992). The third issue which complicates the reception process of Habermas's work is that some of his major early writings have only just been translated. It would be an overstatement to say that English-speakers have received his books in a reverse sequence to that in which they were actually written. But it is true that because the serial appearance of Habermas's work has been uneven and occasionally reversed in English, this has had some significant effects.

We need, therefore, to begin at this beginning, with a sketch of the content of Habermas's books as they have appeared in English, in order to establish some ground for the controversies which have occurred in response to his views. The second section of this essay accordingly provides a summary of Habermas's works. The third sketches some of the controversies more directly, adding a more critical perspective to the reconstructive. The fourth section offers some comments by way of a conclusion.

Habermas in translation

Habermas's major works as they have appeared in English are as follows:

- *Toward a Rational Society*, German 1968–69, English 1970
- *Knowledge and Human Interests*, German 1968, English 1971
- *Theory and Practice*, German 1968, English 1973

- *Legitimation Crisis*, German 1973, English 1975
- *Communication and the Evolution of Society*, German 1976, English 1979
- *Theory of Communicative Action*, volume one 1981, English 1984, volume two 1981, English 1987
- *The Philosophical Discourse of Modernity*, German 1985, English 1987
- *On the Logic of the Social Sciences*, German 1967, English 1988
- *The Structural Transformation of the Public Sphere*, German 1962, English 1989
- *Moral Consciousness and Communicative Action*, German 1983, English 1990.

This is by no means the whole of his work, which extends further into various volumes of essays, uncollected essays in journals, interventions in newspapers, interviews, and so on. But it does suggest some sense of the scope of the project. Let us enter the labyrinth.

Habermas's intellectual project stretches back into the 1950s. His earlier work included critical essays on Marx, the Marx-industry, freelance journalism, and work on the rationalisation of industry and of human relationships (Dews, 1992:187). With the 1960s came the radicalisation of the universities, in Germany as elsewhere. The volatility of this period has frequently been observed. It reminded many of the Weimar Republic, when radicalisation took students off to the political extremities of both right and left, and it sometimes became difficult to distinguish between the two. Socialists, in the interwar years, had after all on occasion become national socialists or national bolsheviks, and fascists agreed in some respects with bolsheviks; both sought alternatives to bourgeois culture, and often to parliamentary democracy. Marxism then travelled east, became the state ideology of the Soviet Union, and transmuted into communism, not least of all for Germans across the Berlin Wall. Into the 1960s enthusiasms spread for the renewal of a libertarian Marxism, a Marxism that would turn against industrialism as well as upon capitalism. Herbert Marcuse became the major prophet of this trend, arguing (as had Adorno and Horkheimer) that modern society was irredeemably flat, one-dimensional, and itself totalitarian

(Marcuse, 1964). Although Habermas's intellectual formation was also dominated by the shadow of Nazism, his response was less pessimistic. Fascism was to him a political turn rather than part of an irreversible historical trend to global decadence. 'Never again!' This is the maxim that frames Habermas's project, and leaves it with the residual optimism that holds up modernity as a project yet to be fulfilled.

Toward a Rational Society (1970) anticipated many themes which would later become motifs of his work. Students could be politically active in ways that the workers' movement could not so readily be; this anticipated the later enthusiasm for social movements. But this recommendation also pinpointed a difficulty anticipated by Max Weber, namely that the politicisation of the universities could also be dangerous. These problems ran along with larger trends, such as the scientisation of politics and of public opinion. Modernity cut both ways; it expanded the space for freedom and democracy, and at the same time took it away. Habermas thus picked up on Adorno's fear that the greatest achievement of modernity would be its rational domination of nature, but added that human action also formed technology (Habermas, 1971:88). The rationality of domination called for analysis of symbolic interaction. Labour, in other words, was like technology, and never more than part of the human story; there was also praxis, and practical philosophy. Culture needed now to be theorised alongside power, and in its own terms. Marxism, traditionally, had worked upon the premise that the key to explaining bourgeois society lay in the critique of political economy (Habermas, 1971:101). But where Adorno had constructed an image of the culture industry as unilaterally determining, and closing off social options, Habermas coupled this argument with a sense of contingency. If the working class was now locked into welfare capitalism, it could not be argued that the social system would merely reproduce the status quo indefinitely. For human beings also have the capacity to learn.

Habermas still insists to this day that he is a Marxist. This is an interesting badge. Partly it can be understood as political, in the everyday sense; partly there is a substantive sense in which Habermas remains committed to sections of the Marxian *oeuvre*, to its reconstruction and critical intent. In different ways, however,

Habermas had by the 1970s evacuated Marx's theory, treating class and class struggle as no longer central, cancelling out the labour theory of value, and introducing instead his own linguistic turn. These developments became more fully evident in *Knowledge and Human Interests* (1971). Here Habermas develops the sense that language, or rather communicative action, is the vital defining attribute of the animals who call themselves humans. The resonances in the argument run back to Aristotle's notion that human beings are best defined as citizens, city-dwellers. It also evokes Immanuel Kant's answer to the question of what is enlightenment: namely the capacity to be autonomous, which depends on the capacity to speak for oneself. Human beings, for Habermas, are deliberative and democratic animals who are able to modify their practical, social and political arrangements by virtue of their very contingency. Critical theory, in this earlier Habermasian formulation, has the capacity to enlighten societies in the same way that psychoanalysis can be revealing of the self. Emancipation remains the interest which guides the critically oriented sciences (Habermas, 1971:308).

If Kant and the Greeks are at work in the shadows here, the project at this point also looks at least from one perspective like an attempt to rethink and possibly to synthesise Marx and Freud, or at least to rethink and expand Marxism as a social theory which is capable of dealing with work, language and power (ibid.:313). This perception may have been strengthened by the translation of Habermas's next book, *Theory and Practice*, the constituent essays of which precede *Knowledge and Human Interests* by some years. *Theory and Practice* (1973) opens with a reflective introduction on 'some difficulties in the attempt to link theory and praxis', and one of its key essays seeks to situate Marxism as a critique between philosophy and science (Habermas, 1973). Habermas defines discourse as increasingly central, in connection with a consensus theory of truth. The idea of consensus, in turn, rests upon the utopia of an ideal speech situation (Habermas, 1973:19). Knowledge always serves interests; the point, however, is politically to define and articulate those interests. 'Critique' now begins to turn on another pivot, that of 'crisis', and here Habermas begins to anticipate the arguments developed later in *Legitimation Crisis* (1975). At this stage, however, Habermas's terms of reference remain closer to those of Adorno than to the language of systems-theories, and anticipate the possible division of humanity into two newer classes— social engineers, and the inmates of closed institutions (Habermas, 1973:282).

By the middle 1970s, the left and the student movement in Australia and across the Atlantic had revived Marx's interest in political economy, and added to it a newer enthusiasm for critique of the state. It was in this setting that Habermas's *Legitimation Crisis* appeared, a firmer title than the literal translation of the German original (Problems of Legitimation in Late Capitalism). This is arguably Habermas's most programmatic book, for it is more concerned to sketch out a research programme than to convey the results of sociological research. Further, the method echoes not only Marx but also Parsons, for it claims to indicate general attributes of a model of late capitalism which, like the political economy in Marx's *Capital*, would be applicable to all like cases. This argument was in turn to anticipate a broader interest in theories of societal evolution. Increasingly Habermas was working on the frame of general theory.

Legitimation Crisis begins from that formal distinction between system and life-world that was hinted at in Habermas's early work, and which later was to become central to the general diagnosis in his *magnum opus, Theory of Communicative Action* (1984, 1987). The use of the language of crisis is significant. Habermas seeks not only to remind us of the contingency of social forms, but also to multiply Marxist sensibilities concerning crisis. In the old Marxian theorem of capitalist collapse, economic crisis in the base of society leads to collapse in its superstructure. In sympathy now with the idea of the autonomy of social spheres, Habermas begins to propose a multiformity of crises. Crises could occur in political processes in the form of a legitimation crisis, or in everyday life as a motivational crisis. Crisis could even afflict the dominant rationality of a social system. Crisis, in addition, has a necessarily subjective component—it depends on the degree of awareness of social crisis in the life-world (Habermas, 1975). The logical implication of the systems-argument is evident: crises could fuse, spill over from some sub-systems into others (such as health care, say, into politics), but by the same token crises could be screened off from other social sub-systems. Late capitalism was thus simultaneously more stable and yet more fragile than the social formations which preceded it.

More than any other of his books, *Legitimation Crisis* probably increased Habermas's standing with Marxists. It is simultaneously Marxistic, in that it takes political economy seriously, and effectively Weberian, in that it draws attention to problems of organisational principles, politics and ethics. At the same time, it gestures both back to Habermas's earlier concern with developmental psychology, and forward to his enthusiasm for theories of societal evolution. The logic which clips these two interests together is to be found in the sense that there is some kind of homology between the development of individuals and of societies. Habermas here retains a sense of the impending possibility that Adorno's nightmare could still be realised: democracy, today, still contains something latently totalitarian, as it facilitates prosperity without freedom (Habermas, 1975:123). This is only ever half the story, however, because individuals and societies still possess the capacity to learn from the experience of fascism, to develop spheres of autonomy, and to mature personally as well as socially. These concerns became more fully evident in *Communication and the Evolution of Society* (1979). This volume opens with further analysis of language and the speech act, which is significant because, as Habermas seems to ascribe some kind of *telos* or end to individual and social development, so apparently language itself in this view manifests the potential for democratic development. Such claims were later to elicit controversy in works by Jean-François Lyotard and Carol Gilligan, which are discussed in the next section.

The first generation of the Frankfurt School had always taken psychology, and more particularly psychoanalysis, seriously. The centrality of socialisation or internalisation followed directly from the task of seeking to explain the experience of German fascism, which after all was a popular regime, reproduced not only by coercion but also by consent. Moreover, if contradictions in the economic base did not themselves assure the collapse of capitalism or the arrival of socialism, then questions of popular belief, authoritarian populism, narcissism and paternalism all emerged in clearer forms as central to social reproduction. Habermas presumes, following Kant, that there is a path of psychological development which progressively takes individuals from dependence to the maturity of speaking and acting for themselves. As Axel Honneth has suggested, the theoretical problem here may be that Habermas fails to distance himself sufficiently from the categories of Adorno's philosophy, which sets society, always incipiently totalitarian, against alienated individuals. Having evacuated classes and social groups from his theory, Habermas downplays the extent to which social order is arrived at through social struggle (Honneth, 1991:303). Communicative action, in other words, remains relatively abstract; the more Habermas relies upon more global categories of social systems, the less apparent their historically contingent and contested character becomes.

Habermas's concern with problems of moral development conspicuously derives from this concern with autonomy and authoritarianism. 'Never again!' After the trial of the notorious Holocaust supervisor Adolf Eichmann, Habermas's question was obvious. Why do people follow evil? How is authority internalised? The analytical problem, I think, is that Habermas transposes Jean Piaget's categories of psychological development into politics via the work of Lawrence Kohlberg. Piaget's concern was to establish hypothetical arguments concerning stages of child development which would suggest the difference between competencies, say, in number, or sense of space or time. All those who watch the children around them know there is something in this, and that the thirsty or greedy child will take the tall glass filled high on the assumption that it contains more liquid than a tumbler filled low. But can this kind of thinking-in-stages then be transferred straightforwardly into arguments concerning right, wrong and the motivation behind behaviour? Plainly the trigger of authoritarianism remains vital here, for it could easily be argued that those who supported Hitler were immature, rule-governed, and too much concerned to be good. But imaginably this can never be more than part of the story, and it may well be the case that Freud rather than Piaget remains more useful here; for supporters of Hitler were also, among other things, self-interested, terrified of socialists, racist, and even perhaps on occasion high-minded nationalists. To follow such a line of inquiry, however, would be to retain a sense that humans are also ever irrational, or else that they practise a multiplicity of rationalities. As I shall suggest later, this is perhaps the major flaw in Habermas's project: its implication that everything can be explained, and that the purpose of sociology is to annex social theory into systems theory alongside theories of language, method, epistemology and action, so that eventually everything can be covered. For the project is, finally, encyclopaedic, and this is an age increasingly sceptical of the possibility of a grand theory of everything.

Communication and the Evolution of Society marked a further expansion of Habermas's project by introducing the idea of reconstructing historical materialism. This lateral shift is like the one in *Legitimation Crisis*, which is simultaneously for and against or beyond Marx. Viewed as a logical possibility, as a potential research programme, the idea of reconstructing historical materialism makes a great deal of sense. Marx's project could be seen as the critique of capitalism, as the mirror of production, but it can also be read as an anthropological theory of history or of successive social formations. If modernity is best explained in terms of its configurations of power, language and culture, then surely these categories can also be read back, historically, in order to enquire into what has made world history both unitary and different. Again, the problem seems to be a certain elasticity in the concepts, categories or ways of thinking involved. Just as cognitive skills do not directly map out phases of moral development, so too patterns of individual development fail to do more than suggest possible paths of anthropological development. We need to ask why Habermas presumes development as a norm, and also to wonder about the apparent slip between an anthropology of individual development to maturity (Kant) and an anthropology of successive social formations (Marx). All the same, it is difficult not to admire the extent of Habermas's scholarship and the breadth of his curiosity. For here, within the covers of one book, specific contemporary analyses of modern world democracy and the welfare state coexist with longer-term diagnoses of pre-capitalist societies. If Habermas's project is foundationalist, committed to the defence of reason and system, and therefore in this sense modernist, it does not make the basic error (fundamental to much sociology) of imagining modernity to be a complete rupture with tradition.

Within this expanded frame of reference there now appeared Habermas's *magnum opus, Theory of Communicative Action*. This major elaboration of his thinking can be understood among other things as a fresh engagement with the thought of Max Weber. Weber was always a presence in Frankfurt theory; implicitly or explicitly, much of the Critical Theory tradition can be understood as an attempt to rethink the first textual encounter with Weber in Lukács's *History and Class Consciousness* (1923) and their alignment as kindred philosophical spirits by Karl Löwith in *Max Weber and Karl Marx* (1932). Weber had feared, as had Adorno, the domination of modernity by instrumental or calculative reason; the echo in Marx's theory is striking, for he had built *Capital* (1867) upon the sense that commodification is a problem because it violates quality or difference as it quantifies the incommensurable. In either perspective, the horror of modernity is that it is governed by the power of number. For Weber, however, rationality has to be pluralised conceptually; there are always competing rationalities, and this sense of cultural thickness and complexity immediately places Weber and Habermas in a relationship of affinity. Marx and Weber, according to Habermas, share the sense that modernisation is not only about rationalisation but that it is also characterised by differentiation (Habermas, 1984:158).

Yet, as Weber indicates when writing under the influence of Friedrich Nietzsche in *The Protestant Ethic and the Spirit of Capitalism* (1904–05), what is rational from one perspective is irrational from another. Rationality can nevertheless be categorised in different ways, and here Habermas follows the Kantian distinction in Weber's work between different rationalities appropriate to the spheres of science, aesthetics and practical life (Habermas, 1984:240). This means that while Weber floats the possibility of a future 'iron cage' or polar night of icy darkness, he also indicates the counter trend, which leads to systemic differentiation (Habermas, 1984:248). Weber is taken up here less as a negative philosopher of history (in the manner of Adorno) than in terms of the theory of action. Action can be instrumental, and oriented either to the technical fulfilment of goals already indicated, or towards articulation of goals that people agree to be desirable. This then returns us to discourse, speech, speech acts, and to the rules and games of language and communication. The possibility of communicative action knocks out even the theoretical possibility of either the totally administered society (Adorno) or the carceral society (Foucault). Habermas turns at this point away from Critical Theory and toward alternative sources in social theory—to Margaret Mead and Emile Durkheim and Parsons—before closing his work by returning to Marx via Weber. This is to reclaim the realm of symbolic interaction, before turning to the deeper distinction between system and life-world. Now Habermas's early concern with the technologisation of society is reinterpreted. The risk today is that the system, economy, administration, threaten to colonise the life-world; in a different language, the argument might be that public colonises private. In other words, a process is going on around us that consistently works against the idea of the integrity of different spheres of existence, each with its appropriate modes of conduct or ways of thinking. Systemic rationalisation—modernisation, in a word— flattens out difference by working against the communicative rationality of the life-world.

Habermas sociologises the still essentially philosophical concept of the impending totalitarian or administrative society feared by the first generation of Frankfurt theorists. The life-world, that realm where sociability and personal politics prevail, always risks invasion by the administrative mentality which these days stands in for politics. There is, of course, nothing wrong with administration or accounting, but they need to be kept in their place. When it comes to the life-world, the argument should be moral and ethical, not simply concerned with output or efficiency. To use a different language, Habermas is deeply apprehensive about the increasing domination of the modern world by number. In this sense he remains a classicist, dedicated to the idea of harmony in proportion.

This critical inflection is carried within, and perhaps obscured by, a richly open and inclusive discussion of various texts in social theory and observations in anthropological works. The extent of Habermas's immersion in the classics of sociology is indicated by his insistence that 'no theory of society can be taken seriously today if it does not at least situate itself with respect to Parsons' (Habermas, 1987:199). Here he echoes the maxim credited to Max Weber that the minimum entrance requirement for discussing the modern condition consists in taking up some attitude to Marx and to Nietzsche. The twist in the Weber aphorism is sharper, however, for anybody who reads Marx may well dismiss Nietzsche, while those who take on Nietzsche will inevitably dismiss Marx. What seems at first sight like an arrogance in Habermas, however, may find its justification in the claimed difference between orders of discourse, for this is a matter of social science, and not politics. Only then would we still have to deal with Marx's plea that there ought not be two sets of rules, one for science and one for life. In the academy, we should certainly expect that all voices or texts have a right to be heard, but the politicisation of the liberal arts, for better or worse, seems to suggest that the culture of tolerance is becoming less likely these days. Appropriately enough, this is the scenario to which Habermas returns in closing—the question whether the colonisation of the life-world by the system does not face us, after all, as the fixed fate of an iron cage. System-rationality may not yet have submerged the rationality of action, but it certainly threatens to do so (Habermas, 1987:333). Social movements now emerge as potential counterbalances. Habermas seems here to underwrite the early–mid 1980s enthusiasm for that 'new politics' which looked, indeed, like a potential extension of the student radicalism of the 1960s.

But as Honneth indicates, this is not the best-developed dimension of the Habermas project. The unfolding of Habermas's work from the 1960s to the 1980s seems to indicate some process of increasing textual complexity and abstraction (Honneth, 1991). In his theoretical work, Habermas gives progressively more attention to systems-models and to textual argument; he continues his political writing in journalism and public work, leaving the theoretical elaboration to proceed as formal and social scientific treatises. English speakers have received far more of the latter.

One biographical peculiarity of this story is the way in which Habermas, who is in effect not only the leading but also the lone Frankfurter of the second generation, sketches out a research programme sufficiently ambitious to occupy an institute. Unfortunately, however, there is no institute, and what remains is a series of hints and insistences as to what might need to be done in order to reconstruct social theory or sociology. Habermas successfully twists

Critical Theory away from philosophy and turns it towards sociology, but the closer analysis of social texture and contestation suggested simultaneously by history or politics seems to escape from his work.

Single-handedly, as it were, Habermas now takes on postmodernism, defending the project of modernity against its detractors. *The Philosophical Discourse of Modernity* was initially a set of lectures. This has probably become Habermas's most widely read and most caricatured book. The problem, however, is not entirely the jaundiced reception it has elicited from academics who identify social theory with French deconstruction or postmodernism. There are two essential aspects to Habermas's critical project. One is to establish a critical distance from postmodernism in order to distinguish between modernity and modernism, to defend modernity as a field of possibility, and to set postmodernism against the background of its predecessors in Romanticism or antimodernism. Habermas's sense of tradition, however, gets in the way. For the second component of his attack on postmodernism involves the reduction of its various arguments to their alleged precedents. Derrida, Foucault, and (implicitly) the absent Lyotard all become 'new conservatives', a category which conceals at least as much as it reveals.

If we glance back momentarily to Weber's aphorism concerning Marx and Nietzsche, some of the issues involved here begin to fall into relief. Habermas does indeed stand in Marx's shadow, in the way that Nietzsche shades the figure of Michel Foucault. Interesting as it might be to read these opposed thinkers against one another, they nevertheless face in different directions. Marx thinks totality, Nietzsche the fragment; Marx looks to the Rousseau who sees the light, Nietzsche to the Freud who tells of the wolf in men. Marx is effectively a humanist, Nietzsche a nihilist. What is unfortunate in the stand-off between the warring theoretical titans of Paris and Frankfurt is that these tensions or contradictions are also those which others, like Weber, struggled to shape into half-truths.

In a sense, Habermas attacks the French with such vehemence because they are repeating what Adorno said from his position of paternal privilege, namely that the world is beyond improvement if not understanding, that democracy is a bad joke, that the entire

Kantian hope of human and social improvement had been buried with Hitler if not before, and that we should stay home and lock the doors. The limit of this debate is that it becomes too readily stylised and distorted, for in effect each side tells only half of the story. For Habermas, the French case rests so heavily on negation and denial that it misses the obvious: we can be outraged by barbarism only because we live in an Enlightenment culture. Whereas the French think that modernity, like socialism, has had its chance and failed, for Habermas it is the failure which represents the challenge. We are not, on his account, postmoderns; if we are, then postmodernity is only the name for a modernity grown conscious of itself. Habermas's purpose is to reintroduce the tension, the vital sense that modernity involves gains and losses. In this sense, Habermas aspires to follow Walter Benjamin's acute sensibility in his *Theses on the Philosophy of History*, that there is no document of civilisation which is not at the same time a document of barbarism (Benjamin, 1968:256). Where the French (from their position of privilege) deny modernity's achievement, Habermas affirms it; he does so too heartily, whether for rhetorical or for other reasons. Modernity, of course, creates more spaces and opportunities for some people than others; democracy is always constrained by asymmetrical relations of power. Needless to say, although Habermas knows all this, it does not figure centrally in his argument, which remains old European. Indeed, while his social theory remains framed by the Holocaust, it lacks a stronger informing sense that there is always an underground, that suffering always accompanies the achievement of modernity, and that different actors experience these phenomena in a more thoroughly positive or negative way (Beilharz, 1994).

Habermas's stance, then, is to oppose the opposition, be they postmodernists or post-structuralists. This reflects his own sense of politics and political engagement. For while Habermas calls himself a Marxist, he also describes his position as social democratic, or 'solidaristic', and the ambiguity is less apparent in Germany where the two have been historically intertwined. What this means is that Habermas sees us and himself as inhabiting and defending a culture or a mainstream, rather than being outside it. While he may be too jaundiced towards nay-saying intellectuals, who after all are not outsiders but also privy to the best spoils of civilisation, he may also give too scant regard to the underworld they claim to inhabit or to represent. This is where Nietzsche stands in the door, for he is the greatest of nay-sayers, the original philosopher-Antichrist and antihumanist. With Nietzsche, Habermas places Heidegger, whose work he considers distracting but whose commitment to Nazism he finds impossibly objectionable. His critique of Heidegger is telling. 'What is irritating is the unwillingness and the inability of this philosopher, after the end of the Nazi regime, to admit his error with as much as *one* sentence—an error fraught with political consequences' (Habermas, 1987:155). Habermas's response is striking because it is constructed so plainly in the language of moralism and rationalism. What Habermas refers to as Heidegger's fascist 'error' seems to indicate that for Habermas, Heidegger's politics could easily have been different. But they were not, as they were not for very many Germans who were anti-Semitic or happy to see strong leaders or high levels of employment. For a leftist or a democrat there is no argument about Nazism. But modernity is also inhabited by various others, who will never share these critical premises or conclusions.

Perhaps it is less than surprising that the French philosopher who fares best in this attack is Foucault. Certainly, in his later years, Foucault drifted back towards the Kant of 'What is Enlightenment?'. As Habermas indicates, this mix is also evident in Foucault's work on psychiatry, where a 'double movement of liberation and enslavement' is described which Foucault later traces along a broad front in various reforms of the penal system, the educational system, the health establishment, social welfare and so forth (ibid.:246). Unfortunately Foucault then loses the sense of balance between the bright and dark sides of enlightenment, just as Horkheimer and Adorno did before him. Where Foucault attacks humanism as a mask for disciplinary power, Habermas defends humanism against power. But certainly a sense of Habermas's engagement with Foucault is discernible, whereas others (like Lyotard, about whom Habermas has stronger reservations) are all but absent from the text.

Habermas closes *The Philosophical Discourse of Modernity* by returning to the defence of his own position, namely communicative or intersubjective rationality. The contemporaneity of his argument with the French was then punctuated awkwardly, this time by the English translation of his much earlier contribution to the philosophy of social sciences. *On the Logic of the Social Sciences* (1988) had first appeared in 1967; those trapped within the English language would only now trace back his apparently more arcane arguments with Karl Popper, Hans Albert, Carl Hempel and Ernest Nagel. More significantly, 1989 saw the final translation of Habermas's first and arguably his best book, *The Structural Transformation of the Public Sphere* (1962). Where the *Logic of the Social Sciences* filled a gap for those choosing to follow the trajectory of Habermas's work, *The Structural Transformation* met a more urgent need. Its publication was to coincide with renewed political and scholarly enthusiasm for the very idea of the public sphere. Its translation, of course, coincided with the collapse of communism. But through the 1980s socialism as a separate dynamic was also unwinding. People no longer spoke, as they did in the early 1980s, of a crisis of Marxism. The idea of socialist politics itself had collapsed. Social movements were widely enthused about as potential social forces which might fill the void left by the further rationalisation of electoral politics and the workers' movement. There was revived talk of civil society, and a renewed desire to identify socialism as democracy (Arato and Cohen, 1992; Keane, 1988).

These were incomplete developments, and they were not always coherent. For after all, if socialism is really about democracy, then why not own up and call it that? And so too social movements lost the lustre which disappointed socialists had first put upon them. The really positive facet of the arrival of Habermas's book was different, for it signalled not only the rediscovery of politics but also what Habermas was pleading for so strongly in *The Philosophical Discourse of Modernity*, namely a rethinking of the negative claims in *Dialectic of Enlightenment*. *The Structural Transformation of the Public Sphere* had begun as Habermas's postdoctoral work. Adorno was disinclined to support it, and so eventually it was overseen by the labour historian, Wolfgang Abendroth. The logic of Habermas's thesis is exactly to put an unwelcome emancipatory twist on *Dialectic of Enlightenment*, by treating its image of modernity-as-closure as not the whole story. Not that the long-term consequence of Habermas's thesis violates Adorno's; rather its message is that the public sphere had flourished briefly in bourgeois form in the epoch of the great revolutions, only to be smothered through colonisation by instrumental reason, and especially by its modern media forms. This reading is structured within the frame of what today would be called historical sociology, for the text discusses the particular forms, strengths and weaknesses of the public sphere as they emerged historically in England and France. Now the work in *Legitimation Crisis* fell into different relief. For here was explained the very appearance of a public agenda which social actors could endeavour to influence; thus Habermas delineates the long road from the French Revolution to the welfare state. Similarly the often dense discussion of speech and language takes on a different kind of urgency, for the public sphere is where talk becomes transformed into politics. And in the meantime there had been a dramatic expansion of discussion about public and private spheres, which made the arrival of the English text even more timely.

Moreover, the book on the public sphere upheld essentially the same claims for the recognition of modernity as did Habermas's attack on recent French philosophy. Enlightenment was to be understood as a project yet to be fulfilled; democracy had hung up its claims, but modernity had yet to deliver adequately. Similarly with the public sphere. Facilitated yet compromised by its bourgeois actors, the public sphere nevertheless posited the value of open participation, even if it did not fulfil it. This is the core of Habermas's politics as a critical theorist working from within society against society's unfulfilled claims, and through critical affirmation rather than negation. As earlier Marxists would have put it, the situation is obvious: if the bourgeoisie offer you freedom, demand it! If they do not deliver, then continue to demand it! For alongside the progressive disappointment of modernity is the ongoing promise of freedom within it. The public sphere, in short, represented an opening, and could always become more open.

Habermas thus discusses here all manner of pertinent detail—family forms, the organisation of house-design, publication of journals and letters, public opinion. To identify the public sphere as bourgeois was also to suggest its inner contradiction. As Marx had understood, because bourgeois ideology still persisted in presenting a particular interest as the general will, there was another opening for political argument in the cleavage between claim and reality. If Marx was prepared finally to dismiss all this talk about citizenship, Habermas wants to pick up the baton and pass it on. Marx, like Foucault, was struck by the fraudulence of the offer; Habermas, more like the social democrats, seeks rather to insist that it be cashed in. Mass media and the culture industry then arrive, with different purposes; the world eventually fashioned by the mass media becomes a public sphere in appearance only. Critical debate and participatory democracy effectively evaporate as their promise is offered.

Habermas's thesis gestures in the direction of Marcuse's one-dimensionality, but its conception picks up on the aspect of arguing for democracy. This is made apparent, for example, in the massive volume of critical responses entitled *Habermas and the Public Sphere* (Calhoun, 1992). This is a remarkable collection, not least because it opens up spaces within which feminist critics and historians set out to extend Habermas's work by establishing the relation between masculinity and the public sphere via (for example) discussion of the work of Joan Landes on the issue of maternal citizenship in the French Revolution (Calhoun, 1992:199). Argument returns here to the realms of politics, contingency, action and social history. The generosity of Habermas's own response to these various arguments is one thing. The other, broader point of significance in this reception-in-reverse, where the first book shall be last, is that it suggests something of the fecundity of the project first anticipated in 1962.

Habermas in dispute

Habermas's response in debate is not always so tolerant as his response to Calhoun and his writers suggests. In *The Philosophical Discourse of Modernity*, as I suggested above, Habermas seems to respond in kind, perhaps as the rules of rhetoric dictate, when it comes to critiquing of the one-dimensional construction or rejection of modernity. That is why his engagement with Foucault is more sympathetic. But if Habermas is a theorist with a project—to defend the idea of communicative action, and to construct around it various supporting sub-theories of language, social science, evolution and crisis—then his is also, as Robert Holub shows, a responsive position. His arguments about social science were formulated in controversy. He has participated in various other controversies: with Gadamer on hermeneutics, tradition and prejudice, with Luhmann on systems theory and the place of social action, and against the revisionist historians of fascism as well as against the French philosophers (Holub, 1991). The most striking aspect of his public disputes with Gadamer and Luhmann is that they seem to obscure the way in which Habermas also accommodates substantial parts of their views in his theory. As regards hermeneutics, Habermas cultivates a method of reading which places tradition in a sympathetic light, and suggests a circular interpretation of the conceptual constellations which form the projects of others. The idea of a consensus theory of truth also suggests the significance of conversation as a model on which both theories rest. With reference to systems theory, Habermas may reject Luhmann's indifference towards, say, democracy, in the same way as he refuses Gadamer's defence of the idea of prejudging, but especially after *Legitimation Crisis* the image of system and sub-system is ubiquitous. As far back as his early work, and culminating in the *Theory of Communicative Action*, his theory is held together by the warring co-ordinates of system and life-world.

About other aspects of thinking incorporated into his theory, Habermas is more defensive. Earlier I referred to his extension of Piaget's schema of cognitive development via Kohlberg into a theory of moral development. This he defends internally, and not least of all against the significant criticism of Kohlberg by Carol Gilligan in her book, *In a Different Voice* (Gilligan, 1982). The implication of Gilligan's book, to simplify, is that Kohlberg's theory of development is a story for boys. The maturing subject reaching post-conventional, universal-rights morality may be a masculine construction, but this is not necessarily the pattern followed by women. In other words, patterns of motivation, justification and action may be different for men and women. Kohlberg's logic, on this basis, conceptually backs women into 'immaturity'. While there has been a great deal of controversy and even methodological debate over these claims, the response of Habermas in his most recent English-language book, *Moral Consciousness and Communicative Action* (1990), is technically dismissive. Habermas acknowledges that there is some empirical or moral difficulty in the implication, following Kohlberg, that by strict definition more than half the American population is morally immature (Habermas, 1990:175). According to Habermas, Gilligan fails to recognise that the question of whether what I ought to do is the same as what I would do concerns only the motivational and not the cognitive problem of mediation (ibid.:179). Viewed from outside, this distinction hardly seems devastating. In general, Habermas here speaks as though those who take on Kohlberg do so in order to supplement the idea of moral stages. The final logic of Gilligan's book, however, is to place the whole idea of moral stages under question. One need not accept the implication that difference works dualistically and across gender lines in order to follow the point. The message may not be that men and women by definition think differently, but rather that different people do. Habermas simply rehearses Kohlberg's insistence that his proposed stages of moral development form an 'invariant, irreversible, and consecutive sequence of discrete structures' (ibid.:127). If one steps outside these strictures, which after all belong to a research programme and not to the sphere of everyday life, the power of the argument is somewhat diminished, as are its clichéd premises regarding the alleged capacities and competences of the adult and the child. If Habermas's argument is thus to be viewed as 'old European', then so be it. So much the worse for children, and other outsiders.

The invisibility of Lyotard in Habermas's *Philosophical Discourse* has already been remarked upon. All the more strange it seems, on reflection, for Lyotard (more so than, say, Foucault) is plainly Habermas's opponent in this debate. What is at risk between them? Lyotard strikes the first blow in *The Postmodern Condition* (1984), where he wickedly constructs Habermas as the professor, as though he himself were not one also. But the postmodern is often characterised as an attitude, and it is 'attitude' which sets French against German. The tension between them can easily be imagined in caricature or cartoon; each sub-system or addition which Habermas seeks to add to his theoretical edifice is for Lyotard, the joker, just another balloon ready to be pricked. Habermas, like Goethe before him, believes truth to be a norm, an orienting device, even if it can never be achieved. In this sense, Habermas's is a hermeneutic of suspicion; more like Foucault, here, Habermas seeks to unmask, whereas Lyotard hopes to deflate. Against the hermeneutics of Gadamer, however, Habermas wants to insist that there is some relation between truth and method; prejudice, authority and tradition must all be brought under rational scrutiny. Gadamer's refusal of this strategy reflects among other things his own romanticism (Gadamer, 1975). Lyotard, similarly, shows up on Habermas's screen as romantic and relativistic. Where Habermas's view of language is oriented to the utopia of consensus, Lyotard's argument begins and ends with dissension. Lyotard's is an agonistic theory of language; Habermas's is a progressive one (Holub, 1991). Lyotard's postmodern world is filled by the languages of the Tower of Babel; Habermas's image is of conversation without intimidation. Needless to say, the logic of Lyotard's position already presumes difference and dispute, and therefore casts Habermas as the opponent if not the enemy. Lyotard's premise is to presume that arguments will always differ and remain beyond resolution. And here the shadow in the background is Freud's: man is a wolf to man.

The possibility that the disagreement between Lyotard and Habermas might be less severe is difficult to see. This is more emphatically the case because Lyotard seems to interpret Habermas's claims about the possibility of consensus as real rather than normative, which is in effect to accuse Habermas of ignoring the effects of power or violence on practices in culture or language (Holub, 1991:142). As is the case with the use of Kohlberg's stages of moral development, Habermas's obvious riposte is that the utopia of undistorted communication does not describe any existing state of affairs, but is heuristic, part not of a political programme but of a thought-experiment. The equally obvious reply which one can imagine from Lyotard is that distinctions between the factual and the counterfactual are hard to preserve. By way of response, Habermas in turn would probably refer to the necessity of philosophical universals in thinking. We can recognise that we will never achieve democracy or freedom in anything other than a nominalistic sense, but we cannot live without these norms as social goals. They facilitate processes of discernment and judge-ment, and help us to decide and to act.

Habermas in conclusion

In comparison with this kind of romantic argument (if that is a reasonable description of Lyotard's position), Habermas's stance is rather classicist, or at least works within and out of tradition. Frankfurt theory was indeed that already, enmeshed as it was in German thinking, whether that of Marx, Weber or Nietzsche. However, after its initial development in a more conventionally sociological pattern of research, the idea of Critical Theory became identified with Adorno's cultural pessimism. Frankfurt took a philosophical turn, a turn towards negation. Habermas's difficult purpose, in this setting, was to seek tentatively to direct Frankfurt out of this impasse by reforming it as a sociology. In this way, his turn to Parsons is objectionable only in the sense that it duplicates Parsons' own slide from a leading concern with a theory of action to a residual focus upon structure or system (Parsons, 1937; 1951). The difference between Parsons and Habermas, however, remains conspicuous. It centres on the figure of Marx. Marx arguably was accepted into American sociology only in the later 1960s; Parsons was no exception in this. Habermas, by contrast, effectively starts with Marx and always returns to him, however sobered he may be by encounters with less fully redemptive thinkers. The common sense of Marxist culture tells us that, even in his own lifetime, Karl Marx insisted that he was no Marxist. Habermas, instead, refuses to break with this claim to tradition. In the 1990s his interest may no longer be in what earlier were called 'theory' and 'practice', but he remains committed both to explaining and criticising the world, and to arguing for its humanisation or radical change.

How might Habermas and Critical Theory then be assessed? The logic of my argument is that Jürgen Habermas has been working both in and against the Frankfurt School. Horkheimer and Adorno knew this, which was one reason why there emerged some distance between them. The first generation of Frankfurters followed Marx and lived with the collapse of Marxist hope. In their lifetimes, Marxism became a state ideology of an eastern imperialism, while the German culture (which among other things claimed philosophy for itself) also incubated Nazism. Habermas's challenge was to register these ruptures, and to reform them in a philosophy where hope and reason might be recombined. Second-generation Critical Marxism, however, was to coincide with the emergence of mass tertiary education, which both encouraged the student radicalism of the 1960s and served to enmesh Marxism with the academy rather than with the organisations of the workers' movement. Marxism's insertion into this critical culture also stood for incorporation into the practice of social theory in a broader sense. But as a sociology, Marxism as critical theory became increasingly general and abstract.

As Helmut Dubiel argues, the perspective taken up by critical theory, focusing on domination in the first generation and emancipation in the second, also brings with it an attitude, the former more given to resignation, the latter to hope. In this sense, the two most significant texts of the longer Critical Theory tradition are *Dialectic of Enlightenment* and *Theory of Communicative Action*. The first generation of Critical Theory, oriented primarily toward a theory of domination, is mainly concerned with the mechanisms by which individuals reproduce their condition of submission. The second generation, in contrast, is largely interested in the idea of the emancipatory potentials of individuals and groups (Dubiel, 1992). The earlier version of Critical Theory draws attention to conformism; the later version constructs domination as a human as well as social phenomenon.

Attention might now turn to the prospect of a third generation of Critical Theory, of which Axel Honneth is the most prominent member. Honneth's first major work, *Critique of Power* (1991), is among other things a settling of accounts with Critical Theory, which is engaged by way of a critique of Horkheimer, Adorno, Habermas and Foucault. In summary, Honneth's view is that Critical Theory originally involved an attempt to supplement the critique of political economy by adding psychoanalysis as the superstructure. Entering this edifice, Habermas effectively takes on the same task, replacing Freud with Piaget and Kohlberg and adding various other supports as sub-theories which are either logically foundational or supplementary. What recedes, or remains marginal in this process, is that struggle for resources and recognition which makes the social edifice possible (Honneth, 1991). Honneth's case thus runs in parallel to that of Alain Touraine's request for a 'return of the actor' (Touraine, 1987). The research implications of this critique point in two different directions at the same time. First of all, it is now necessary (so to speak) to add the dimension of 'internal' colonisation (within nation states) to that of colonisation of the life-world by system. Asymmetrical relations of power are ubiquitous, especially after Keynesian economics and globalisation; talk of autonomy and democracy needs now to proceed in this frame of recognition. Second, future outcomes of societal evolution ought now to be viewed in terms of that struggle for recognition which is primary to human existence.

Habermas's great contribution to Critical Theory is to turn it in this direction, even if his own theory then fails to ground it sufficiently in the way in which Honneth recommends. Habermas's theory is therefore paradigmatic of the development of ideas—able to recognise the problems it faces even if it cannot always solve them, and opening up new possibilities for those who would be so bold as to stand on the shoulders of giants. As far as Habermas is concerned, it can truly be said that no serious thinker or critic in the liberal arts today can avoid taking a position on his work. The challenge of a critical theory remains before us.

4

Niklas Luhmann and the Theory of Social Systems

Paul R. Harrison

The work of Niklas Luhmann represents the most developed and most radical attempt within contemporary sociology to recast completely the theory of society. It is the most developed because no other body of work has pursued its guiding theoretical idea so completely through the various systems of modern society that it has identified. It is the most radical because no other body of work has taken up a particular theoretical inheritance and developed it with such rigour and originality. These characteristics of Luhmann's work are not a product of subjective accident; they result from his attempt to revolutionise the theory of society by moving partly outside the sociological inheritance. In Luhmann's view, the resources of the sociological tradition have mainly exhausted themselves, and their further deployment can result only in unimaginative recycling operations. The strategy, therefore, is to open up sociology to the outside, but in a vastly different way from those who would submerge it into a generalised practice of deconstruction. For Luhmann, the under-explored theoretical resource of systems theory constitutes the outside to which sociology needs to open up, and into which society—redescribed as 'the societal system'—will be embedded. Of course, this is not the first time that sociology has used systems theory to revolutionise itself. The most celebrated former instance is the work of a major sociological influence on Luhmann, namely the American sociologist Talcott Parsons. Yet Luhmann's work is the first and most ambitious attempt to exploit the theoretical resources of the new systems theory, and to redescribe the social system in the light of its concept of 'autopoiesis' or self-production.

Redescribed with the aid of systems theory, 'society' scarcely resembles what it is taken to be in both the western tradition and contemporary sociology. For Luhmann, 'society' as *koinonia* or *societas* has been seen within the western tradition as a part of a more encompassing whole called 'political society' (*koinonoia politiké* or *societas civile*) (Luhmann, 1990a:175). Such a view of society, according to Luhmann, is possible only within a centred and stratified society where a politically defined elite co-ordinates social life. With the advent of modernity, and the emergence of a decentred and functionally differentiated social system, the political process no longer occupies the centre of social life, and no other social process can take its place. Hence the Marxist theorem concerning economic determination in the final instance is rejected as well as anthropological theorems about cultural determination. From the point of view of systems theory, the more encompassing whole is now seen as society or the societal system, defined as the sum total of meaningful internal communication; what formerly were the parts are now construed as particular social systems, which are highly specific forms of meaningful communication (ibid.:176). The encompassing societal system, therefore, observes and regulates communications through communication. Its operational closure by and through communication means that it cannot communicate with other non-communicational systems that constitute its environment, such as machines, organisms and psyches (Luhmann, 1985a:16). Social systems are highly coded forms of particular communication that arise out of the functionally differentiated nature of modern, complex societies. The economy, the law, politics, science, religion and education are, for Luhmann, so many social systems. They demarcate themselves from their respective environments through the ways in which their internal forms of coding both close them off operationally from their respective environments and differentiate them internally from other social systems. The deconstruction of inherited theories of society and its systems-theoretical reconstruction is the guiding idea that underlies Luhmann's reconception of the functionalist tradition in sociology.

This chapter is an analysis of systems theory and Luhmann's use of it, since these form the indispensable basis for any discussion of Luhmann's work. I begin by distinguishing Luhmann's early use of cybernetic forms of systems theory from his later use of those more advanced forms of systems theory (developed within biology) that rest on the notion of autopoiesis. I then turn to Luhmann's social theory, which I characterise as both functionalist and evolutionist, and survey Luhmann's work within the sociology of knowledge, particularly his reconstruction of the emergence of romantic love. I try to show how Luhmann's systems theory deals with such contemporary topics as the ecological movement, the future of democracy, risk perception and globalisation. At this point alternative paradigms in the social sciences are used to critique Luhmann's theory of social systems, and with respect to three main issues: systems theory versus action theory; evolutionism versus anti-evolutionism; and constructivism versus critical theory and deconstruction. I conclude with a few remarks on the paradoxical achievements of Luhmann's systems-theoretical transformation of sociology.

Systems theory

One of the great oppositions within sociology has been that between action and structure. 'Action' has often been modelled either on *collective* action (as in Marx's theory of class actors and class struggle) or on the *individual* act or action-event, as in Weber's theory of subjectively meaningful action. Structure has been construed as both supra-individual and constraining. It either constitutes meaning (in Marx's theory, commodity production gives rise to fetishism) or is itself constituted meaning (as in Durkheim's theory of the *conscience collective* and, more particularly, his later theory of *representations collectives*). This classical dichotomy has given way in recent times to theories of practice, such as those of Pierre Bourdieu and Anthony Giddens, which attempt to articulate both moments in an enlarged theory that sees itself as directed respectively to reproduction or structuration. This is not the strategy, however, that Luhmann follows. He takes his cue from Parsons' life-long theoretical journey away from voluntaristic action theories and towards more functionalistic systems theories. Hence the key theoretical decision to be formulated is not between action and structural theories, but between action and systems theory. The possibility of avoiding such a distinction through a syncretic or unifying theory of practice is rejected in advance. In Luhmann's early work, the traditional concept of action (which arises out of Greek philosophy) is embedded in a means-ends schema: because the ends of action were constructed as being inscribed in nature, the choice of means had to comply with this pre-given substantive concept of rationality (Luhmann, 1973:7–17). With the advent of modernity the substantive concept of nature disappears, and the choice of ends becomes radically subjectivised. This development produces two unsatisfactory outcomes: either an *existentialist* emphasis on the moment of choice or decision (which is an event drained of all rationality), or a *formalist* emphasis on the adequacy of means chosen for any given end which in itself has no particular rationality. The way out of this impasse is, for Luhmann, to abandon action theory for systems theory. Systems theory rescues rationality by reconceiving it as a property not so much of the purposes or ends of action but rather of the social system and the way it functions. More specifically, rationality is seen as what enables social systems to reduce complexity within the environments they operate in. Although Luhmann later reformulated this radically desubjectivised notion of rationality, the core of his programme remains an emphasis on reducing environmental complexity through the enhancement of systemic complexity as a systemic property.

The work of Luhmann falls into two periods. In the 1960s and 1970s Luhmann tries to move beyond the Parsonian inheritance to a more rigorous systems theory in line with current cybernetic theories, while at the same time incorporating a phenomenological account of trans-individual meaning. The 1980s and 1990s see Luhmann reworking his entire theory in the light of recent developments within the biological and cognitive sciences centred on the concept of autopoiesis. The major theoretical work of the first period is to be found in those essays by Luhmann which were published together with Habermas's critical exchanges in a famous volume that initiated a series of further volumes in which other participants took up the respective arguments (Habermas and

Luhmann, 1971). The significance of this work is that Luhmann frees himself from his earlier attempt to rescue purpose or ends as a property of systems, and moves toward a more properly cybernetic concept of systemic selectivity. In his essay on modern system theories in the *Theorie-Diskussion* volume Luhmann reconstructs their history in four stages. In the first stage, systems are understood in terms of the relations between the parts, and between the parts and the whole. The next stage develops equilibrium theories, where the notion of an environment is introduced as a source of disturbance that may or may not be compensated for by a change of systemic state. At the third stage is developed an environmentally-open systems theory, where systems are seen as being in a process of exchange with an environment which they try both to maintain themselves from and selectively steer. The next stage is marked by the development of cybernetic systems theory. It conceptualises the environment within which systems move as overwhelmingly complex, and assigns systems the task of reducing this complexity. By increasing their own ability to handle complexity, the systems themselves become more complex, or create more 'requisite variety'. This enables systems to use increased selectivity in order to reduce environmental complexity (ibid.:10). What this history indicates is that modern systems theory really begins only with the distinction between system and environment. Furthermore, the trend in systems theory is to conceive of this relationship in terms not of interchange but of systemic closure. This trend culminates in autopoietic systems theory, which regards operational closure as a condition of selective openness to the environment.

Luhmann's task in his early work was to develop a cybernetic theory of social systems, starting from the elementary datum of the societal environment, namely 'the social contingency of meaningful lived experience (*Erlebnis*)' (ibid.:11). The task of the social system is to reduce this complexity, and it does this by increasing its own complexity as a 'system which identifies itself through meaning' (ibid.). As a consequence, meaning is no longer a property of a subject or of subjective intention; instead, a subject or subject's act is a property of meaning understood 'as a system that uses meaning' (ibid.:12). Meaning becomes, in this sense, 'a determinate strategy of selective behaviour (*Verhalten*) under the conditions of higher complexity' (ibid.). Meaning is therefore understood by Luhmann in two radically different ways: as lived experience (*Erlebnis*) and behaviour (*Verhalten*). The similarity between these two uses of meaning is just as important as their manifest difference, and resides in the fact that, whether as 'horizon' or 'system', meaning is a trans-individual and deintentionalised phenomenon. The difference here is between Edmund Husserl's idea of meaning as a 'horizon', and the systems-theoretical idea of meaning as 'systemic selectivity'.

The task of a system that uses meaning is to reduce environmental complexity by increasing its own systemic complexity. In modern society, functional differentiation allows for greater systemic complexity, and society becomes therefore more capable of handling environmental complexity. This means that modern society splits up into a number of sub-systems, each of which processes particular systems of meaning. Luhmann gives three brief examples —subsequently turned into books—of how this works (ibid.:16–17). Science deals with statements by processing them as either true or not true. Law deals with decisions that follow from the autonomous logic of positively enacted law. Love becomes a phenomenon of individualised passion, rather than *philia* (an essential part of the ethos of every social system). All these systems work with meaning, and demarcate their boundaries from other systems by the different way they process meaning. As this allows such systems to reduce environmental complexity in a way not possible in premodernity, functional differentiation represents, for Luhmann, an evolutionary development. Evolution means that, in a state of greater environmental complexity, systems are able to increase their capability amidst widening alternatives by increasing their selectivity. This ensures stability, but only at a higher level of complexity (ibid.:22). Hence, the ever-increasing level of possible experience and action (*Erlebnis* and *Handeln*) is countered by the greater systemic selectivity of sub-systems (meaning as selective behaviour or *Verhalten*).

When Luhmann reworked his theory in line with new develop-ments within systems theory, the functionalist and evolutionist aspects of his programme remained intact within a transformed framework. Those innovations emerged outside sociology, which Luhmann accuses of dealing only with either self-produced data or self-produced classics (Luhmann, 1985a:28). The sources of this new systems theory Luhmann locates, on the one hand, in thermo-dynamics, biology, neurophysiology, cell theory and computer theory; on the other hand, in information theory and cybernetics, including second-order cybernetics (ibid.:27). The account that Luhmann now gives of the history of systems theory divides it into three rather than four stages. First comes the ancient concept of the whole and the parts, while the second stage is inaugurated by the concept of environmentally-open systems. The third stage sees the emergence of what Luhmann calls 'self-referential systems theory' which he sets himself the task of developing in terms of social systems (ibid.:20–5). Self-referential systems produce and use descriptions of themselves in order to constitute their elements and their operations. These descriptions are founded on, but go beyond, the systems-internal construction of a distinction between 'system' and 'environment'. Hence, unlike open systems theory (which postulates a simple system/environment distinction), self-referential theory postulates the replication of this distinction within the system itself. Systems are said to be operationally closed, therefore, because they are not in an interchange with an environment; instead, they use the elements of which they are composed to generate their own operations. Consequently they are described as autopoietic. This does not mean, however, that self-referential theory is solipsistic, for according to Luhmann the environment is a necessary correlate of self-referential operations. Yet it does mean that their openness to the environment is produced through their self-referential closure, rather than through a set of input and output mechanisms (ibid.:25). The notion of self-referential closure means that the difference between identity (system) and difference (environment) is prior to any concept of identity (ibid.:26). In this stress on difference—and in the con-comitant stress on the constructed nature of reality as a product of self-referentially closed systems—Luhmann has produced a systems-theoretical pendant to the postmodern celebration of difference and its deconstruction of the identitarian logic of western philosophy.

The idea of the self-referential nature of systems applies equally to social systems, which are conceived of by Luhmann as operatively closed systems of meaningful communication. Society is composed of communication because communications are its basic elements and communicating is its fundamental operation. It can observe and regulate itself only through further communications: as an 'observing system', society observes itself through communications on communications. In brief, it functions autopoietically. As a consequence, society does not communicate with its environment, which becomes visible, according to Luhmann, only in so far as it irritates or disturbs communication (Luhmann, 1989:29). The corollary of this is that society can endanger itself only through communications. Threats to society do not stem from the environment or environmental catastrophe, but from communications about the environment produced by the social system itself (ibid.:32). These are what Luhmann calls *communications of anxiety*.

The sub-systems of society also function self-referentially through their own programmes. These operate communicatively or, more precisely, through binary codings that exclude the possibility of a third alternative. For example, the legal system's programme revolves around justice, which is produced by legal norms that encode actions in terms of their legality or illegality. The economic system focuses on money and money transactions, in which prices operationalise a programme that determines whether or not one can and will pay. The scientific system is centred on the acquisition of new scientific knowledges which take the form of theories that can either be true or false. The democratic political system rests on the production of collectively binding decisions by persons who hold offices or, in sum, possess power. They constitute the government as opposed to the opposition (ibid.:84–94). The artistic system revolves around form, according to which styles and stylistic innovations are coded as either beautiful or ugly (Luhmann, 1990a:191–215). Each of these sub-systems has its own point of self-reference (justice, money, knowledge, power and beauty) and its own programme of autopoietic closure (laws, prices, scientific theories, offices and styles) with which it observes and processes its self-created reality. The sum of these sub-systems no longer constitutes a totality, because there is no longer any unifying point. The position from which these 'observing systems' can themselves be observed is accordingly within, rather than from outside.

Social theory

Luhmann's work belongs to the functionalist school of sociology even as it transforms and radicalises that perspective through its systems-theoretical approach. His main theoretical predecessors are Durkheim and, more immediately, the late work of Parsons. Luhmann rejects the Weberian approach because it takes the individual act and its subjective meaning as its starting point; he rejects the Marxian approach because the idea of social critique requires a position external to society that is quite simply unavailable. He sees no further value in the Durkheimian approach for two reasons. First, despite introducing the theory of social differentiation, Durkheim still saw a connection between newer forms of solidarity and morality that failed to recognise the morally neutral character of symbolic media such as money. Secondly, although it incorporates evolutionism, Durkheim's theory tries to connect evolution with changes in size, and neglects the self-referential character of the process (Luhmann, 1982:3–20). Hence the post-action-theoretical work of Parsons is the immediate influence on Luhmann. Luhmann's strategy is to see elements of a theory of self-reference emerging in Parsons' AGIL schema (adaptation, goal attainment, integration, latent pattern maintenance, in so far as each square could be construed as being operationalised by its own symbolically generalised medium of exchange) (ibid.:62). Hence Luhmann began where Habermas ended, namely with the Parsonian idea of the symbolic media of money and power as systems-organising media. In Luhmann's later work, however, there is a more complex theory of autopoietic closure that redescribes the media hypothesis. There is also a more pluralised description of societal sub-systems that does not play off the life-world against systems of money and power, but instead sees each and every sub-system as possessing its own environment.

As a functionalist analysis, Luhmann's social theory is centred on notions of differentiation and evolution. With respect to differentiation, Luhmann argues in his early work that only a few forms have been developed: segmentation, stratification, and functional differentiation. 'Segmentation' is a feature of 'archaic' societies, where differentiation occurs through the formation of equal sub-systems (as when a tribe reaches the ecological limits of its size, and a new unit splits off). 'Stratification' occurs in what are usually referred to as 'civilised' societies, which differentiate society into distinct or 'unequal' sub-systems. Because equality is seen as residing in one's own society, other societies are constructed as being 'unequal' or 'inferior'. Stratification also occurs in societies where the upper classes treat the lower classes as an unequal sub-system with which they do not communicate (ibid.:233–5). What is significant here is the classification of both ancient democracies and ancient tyrannies as merely different strategies of stratification. Finally, there is 'functional differentiation', which separates functions according to specific communication processes. In this case, argues Luhmann, the functions are 'unequal' or distinct, but access to them has to be equal. The advantage of this form of differentiation is that it handles complexity better (ibid.:236–7). In Luhmann's later work, the sub-systems of a differentiated society are conceived of as Leibnizian monads, each expressing the unity of the system in its own way. No functional system can be substituted for another, even though processes of change (or as Luhmann puts it, substitutions) are internal to each sub-system. This means that although sub-systems may organise themselves differently, the specific *differences* of each one must be retained. The politicisation of the economy or the sacralisation of society would result in an untenable de-differentiation that would sacrifice the benefits brought by modern society (Luhmann, 1989:106–12). Consequently, certain forms of socialism and fundamentalism, as well as ecologism, are construed as anti-modern.

Luhmann's evolutionism puts him outside most of the main currents of modern social theory, which, because of the influence of structuralism and post-structuralism, are determinedly anti-evolutionist. There are two main and interlinked components of Luhmann's evolutionism. First, there is the more general social-theoretical argument that because societies move from being stratified and become functionally differentiated, this represents an evolutionary gain that only processes of de-differentiation can undo. Secondly, an argument from within the sociology of knowledge correlates changes in historical semantics with the change from stratified to differentiated societies. With respect to the first component, Luhmann's evolutionism specifically distinguishes itself from the social Darwinism of its nineteenth-century predecessors, and places itself within the Darwinian tradition proper. What Luhmann is looking for is not some sort of macro-historical and causal theory of the shift from premodern to modern societies, but a theory that uses the language of variation, selection and stabilisation to account for the capacity of modern societies to exercise greater control (Luhmann, 1982:258). As to what makes variation possible in the first place, Luhmann seems to have two different answers. In the early work, the ability of language to say 'no' is the fundamental linguistic fact that makes evolutionary variation or novelty possible (ibid.:266). In the later work, it is the veritable 'research field' of interaction which constitutes the possibility of variation—even though socio-cultural evolution itself presupposes the difference between interaction systems and societal systems, and even though real evolutionary advances are possible only at the level of societal systems themselves (Luhmann, 1985:575). With regard to important variants that have been selected and thereafter stabilised successfully, Luhmann's opinion has also differed. In the early work, he mentions the Greek *polis*, the twelfth- and thirteenth-century territorial reorganisation of Europe, and the development of modern bourgeois society in the eighteenth and nineteenth centuries, all of which are moments when change and reflection on change simultaneously emerge (Luhmann, 1982:267). In his later work there appears to be a two-fold line of argument. One centres on the forms of communication, and looks at new evolutionary developments such as writing and print; it even entertains reflections reminiscent of Jean Baudrillard on the new forms of communication (Luhmann, 1985a:410; 1990a:86–106). The other argument starts from his distinction between interaction and societal systems, with only the latter capable of stabilising more improbable evolutionary forms. These two lines of speculation come together in Luhmann's suggestion that society works communicatively, and that societal sub-systems operate by using forms of coding. Communicatively operational and binary-coded sub-systems represent an evolutionary advance on interaction systems, which emphasise factual, spatial and temporal presence. They do so, according to Luhmann, by allowing for greater abstraction and technical proficiency, and hence a more complex means of handling environmental complexity.

The idea of a process of evolution in the domain of historical semantics is opened up by Luhmann's observation that if reflection on change accompanies change, evolution is not merely material but also socio-cultural. The central field of Luhmann's investigation in this domain is the so-called *Sattelzeit* (Koselleck) or the period of the second half of the eighteenth century. The hypothesis is that at this time our ways of observing or describing society changed. Hence the task of a sociology of knowledge, as reformulated by Luhmann, is to observe the observations, describe the descriptions, and communicate the communications that society makes about itself. For Luhmann, there must be a 'compatibility' between the dominant semantics and the social structure. He therefore rejects Foucault for first rejecting the effect of social structures on discourse, and then falsely construing the effect of discourse on social structure as power. According to Luhmann, a semantics is an apparatus that contains the available stock of rules for processing meaning. The selected or dominant semantic reduces the complexity of potential references by making available (to the individual) a 'high level of generalised and relatively situationally-independent meaning' (Luhmann, 1980:19). Luhmann links semantics to social structures through his theory of evolution, and in particular his idea that the advent of modernity is marked by the development of differentiated symbolic media which are at the core of the sub-systems of modern society. Hence different semantics arise out of the differentiated sub-systems of modern society as they emerge in the late eighteenth century. Luhmann's research project is to investigate such sub-systems as law, politics, religion and education in terms of semantic shifts in their conceptual or observational apparatuses. This involves more general enquiries into changes in temporal horizon or patterns of moral reflection in modernity.

As an illustration of Luhmann's approach to this field I would like to analyse his reconstruction of the three stages in the development of the modern form of 'love as passion' (Luhmann, 1986). These stages represent three different semantic codes for the 'processing' of intimate communication. Luhmann reconstructs these codes out of a reading of the popular (rather than the great) literature of the respective periods, for such sources provide the resources of meaning with which individuals make sense of their experiences and actions. The three codes are those of 'courtly love', *amour passion* and 'romantic love'. The medieval code of courtly love operated on the basis of idealisation. The woman was not an actor but an ideal, as Beatrice was for Dante. Her ideal status was determined by both the inferiority of the lover to the beloved and the metaphysical inferiority of physical to spiritual love. Within the semantic field of the late seventeenth century, however, the form of the code of *amour passion* was determined by paradoxicalisation. Both the woman and the man are now actors in the game of love, and hence the relationship becomes doubly contingent because either can say 'yes' or 'no'. This freedom results in word-play that uses formulae whose meaning is ambiguous or paradoxical, since the game of love extends over time as a mutual projection of each lover's imaginary desires. Given the novelty of the woman's right to decide, however, the code places most importance on the woman's position. Love tends to develop its new semantic within the context of this growing freedom, including the progressive incorporation of sexuality. Love is no longer governed by idealisation, but depends instead on an excessiveness which alone furnishes the proof of love. No longer an ideal frozen in time, it is subject to the vagaries of passing time. The shift to romantic love occurs around 1800 with a shift in the code to self-referentiality. Love becomes its own justification once its complete autonomisation as the sphere of intimate communication is established. As with all symbolic media, 'love as passion' makes more probable a highly improbable form of communication, and in love's case this is called 'personal communication' or 'interpersonal penetration'. With the transformation of love into self-referential communication, the modern risk *par excellence* emerges as a possibility: the subjection of love to the discourses of the therapists of intimate communication.

Issues

Luhmann's approach to the ecological question is a quite remarkable functionalist defence of the complexity of modern society against the totalising claims of the environmentalist movement. It is remarkable for its use of the concept of difference in a way that defends it, by redefining it, against its supposed supporters, who turn out to be the enemies of the redefined concept of difference. Luhmann's definition of difference turns on the conception of society as the sum of its various sub-systems which, in so far as none can represent the whole, is seen as constituting unity in and through difference to form a *unitas multiplex*. The sub-systems themselves are constituted by difference, and it is the difference between system and environment that constitutes the operational difference. For systems theory, society cannot communicate *with* the environment, but only *about* it. Because society is a system of communications, it can only communicate about communications. Luhmann accuses the environmental movement of projecting the friend/foe schema on to the system/environment distinction, and of therefore producing forms of communication that are anxiety-charged, moralistic and irrational. Luhmann admits that ecological problems can create too little resonance, because the various sub-systems react to ecological problems only in terms of their own coding, and therefore tend not to act unless faced with a catastrophe. Nevertheless, the real problem today as he sees it is that in fact they create too much resonance. As ecological problems become over-communicated, communication becomes anxiety-laden. For Luhmann, anxiety-communications have replaced normative discourse as the common form of communication. Consequently it has become a sign of authenticity to demonstrate anxiety. It is precisely these anxiety-ridden communications about the environment that Luhmann sees as creating too much resonance, and therefore threatening society from inside by over-loading it with too many demands. Such communications are also moralistic and polemical, in so far as ecologists construct the situation as a taking of sides with the environment against enemies who represent the system. When these communications enter the political system their velocity increases because, according to Luhmann, they promote 'loose talk': demands to make this or that sub-system yield to ecological needs become commonplace. Finally, such communications are theoretically deficient in self-description. In short, they are not as theoretically sophisticated as socialism was, despite its ultimate utopianism, in projecting a revolutionary dialectic for resolving social difference. Instead their self-observations become, according to Luhmann, either uninterestingly ideological or (in so far as they have any content) *'a protest against functional differentiation and its effects'*: they are anti-difference and anti-modern (Luhmann, 1989:125). The environment is not a macro-subject that can retotalise the differentiated space of modern society. What we are left with, according to Luhmann, is ecological difference (system/environment) as the operative distinction of a differentiated society.

Luhmann's theory of democracy is articulated against both its detractors and its adherents. Against its detractors Luhmann argues that political division or difference is the operative principle of a modern political system, whereas against its adherents he argues for a more realistic assessment. The theoretical construct of dialectics and revolution is one such totalitarian construct, in so far as it constructs revolution as the transcendental leap beyond the dialectics of class division to a society without difference. This defence of democracy borrows from (even as it redescribes) the work of Claude Lefort and Marcel Gauchet on the socially split space of modern politics that only an 'egocrat' with a totalitarian project can spuriously attempt to reunite. Luhmann's argument against democracy is directed against its old European definitions. Democracy, for Luhmann, is neither the rule of the people over the people nor popular participation in decision-making, but instead a splitting or a *'bifurcation of the top'* (Luhmann, 1990c:232). Hence it is unlike premodern political systems, which reflected the unitary class ethos of the dominant stratum in a hierarchically ordered society. The unity of the top is now bisected by a difference; the specific difference that operationalises the political system is the one between government and opposition. One is either in power or out of power; one either holds or does not hold office; one either makes collectively binding decisions, or one does not: in short, one either has or does not have political power. Also essential to democracy, for Luhmann, is that the difference between government and opposition should not be thought of along the lines of friend and foe. This is to prevent political opposition from being constructed as inimical to society, as happened in the United States, for instance, during the McCarthy period of the 1950s. The opposition is Her Majesty's Loyal Opposition, and as such is not excluded from the system. The theoretical advantage of Luhmann's account of democracy is that it enables democracy to be connected to the state by means of a theory that specifies how the electoral mechanisms permit an alternation in the control of state power. Its main theoretical disadvantage lies in the fact that because civil society appears only as the environment of the political system it provides only irritation or resonance. Politics can observe itself in the mirror of public opinion, as Luhmann puts it, only when public opinion is construed not as something 'out there' in the environment but as something used by the system in order to observe itself. 'The mirror of public opinion' makes possible, for Luhmann only 'an *observation of observers'* (Luhmann, 1990d:216). The idea that public opinion is the means by which political actors observe themselves and each other—rather than something out there to which they respond—is shared also by Jean Baudrillard in his postmodern reflections on modern politics. For Luhmann, however, this phenomenon is not something new to which a prefix needs be attached. What is new, if anything, is merely the way in which the phenomenon is being observed through a systems-theoretical approach.

Luhmann's reflections on risk are in many ways an extension of his perspective on the ecological question, in so far as ecological communications are but one form of risk-communication in modern societies. It is also an extension of his critique of the utopianism of critical theory, because his own theory is articulated against that 'critical' perspective on risk which was developed by Ulrich Beck (1992). Luhmann begins by distinguishing 'risk' from 'danger'. Catastrophes have always been with us, according to Luhmann: what is new are catastrophes produced by our own decisions. 'Danger' is harm that is externally produced or environmentally determined, whereas 'risk' involves a harm caused by our own decisions, and is therefore a normal and inevitable product of our attempts to 'bind time' (Luhmann, 1991:30–1). Risk emerges historically, according to Luhmann, in the long transition from the Middle Ages to the early modern period. It operated, significantly enough, in the domain of maritime insurance, although its usage was far more extensive than this economic example would suggest (ibid.:17–18). What this example illustrates, however, is the way in which rationality comes to be construed as the management of harm produced by our own decisions: we try to 'bind time' by calculating in advance the losses we may endure and insuring against them. Of course we can never really know what these losses will be, for we cannot know the future, not even the future produced by our own decisions. But what we can do through the calculation of risk is to install what Luhmann calls (with ironic reference to the confessional) a 'repentance minimisation pro-gramme' (ibid.:19). This way of looking at risk has two important corollaries. The more important is that 'there is no risk-free behaviour', since decision-making (as a mode of binding an unknowable future) brings with it an inevitable risk that cannot be avoided by abstaining from decision-making. The other corollary involves the paradoxical predicament of knowledge: the more we know, the more we know what we do not know, and consequently risk increases rather than decreases with the advance of knowledge. The risk-society of modernity is for Luhmann a product of this predicament, and is not produced (as it is for Beck) by realising the harm that modern technology brings (ibid.:37–8).

The risk-society is also, for Luhmann, a product of modernity rather than of the shift within modernity away from modern class-society to a postmodern risk-society, as it is for Beck. It is not only the etymology of the term 'risk' which suggests this dating, but also transformations in the semantic coding of time into a 'before' and 'after'. Traditionally Europeans divided time according to the distinction between immanence (*tempus*) and transcendence (*aeternitatis*). By contrast, the modern semantic operates with a distinction between 'past' and 'future' in which the future is constructed as inevitably risky (ibid.:41–2). The 'present' in this schema is the standpoint of the non-observable observer; it is the position of the 'excluded middle' or 'parasite' or 'blind spot' whose absent presence makes observation possible. This fact makes the evaluation of risk temporally dependent on the present: risk perception, therefore, is a historically variable phenomenon (ibid.:50–1). Amidst this variability, however, Luhmann sees two evolutionary trends. One of these transforms dangers into risks, and results from ever greater levels of decision-making in the functionally differentiated sub-systems of the modern social world.

The other trend is toward a growing trust in the possibilities of technology and a corresponding distrust in politics (ibid.:54–76). This modernist perspective on risk radically differentiates Luhmann's diagnosis of the politics of contemporary perception from Beck's. For Luhmann, 'there are always decision-makers and those affected', and mechanisms of decision (such as markets, hierarchies and states) inevitably produce and reproduce this distinction (ibid.:115). Accepting the inevitability of this asymmetry, Luhmann ascribes the current loss of authority of decision-makers among those affected by their decisions not to any conjunctural difficulty, but to the logic behind the asymmetry: the risky future produced by the decision-makers' decision must appear to outsiders affected by it as a danger to them (ibid.:118–19). This puts protest movements in the utopian situation of 'rejecting situations in which one can become the victim of the risky behaviour of another', for such situations are inevitable given the distinction between decision-makers and decision-victims (ibid.:146). Instead of the high hopes people like Beck place in protest movements as agents of 'reflexive modernisation', Luhmann sees them as 'watch dogs': they may be able to restore a little order, but they cannot overcome the distinction that creates their position as 'watch dogs' for the affected. Decision-making centres inevitably create risky futures, however much the 'watch dogs' 'bark' and 'bite' (ibid.:154).

Luhmann's reflections on globalisation do not seem to be as developed as his work on other topics. This appearance is due to the fact that 'globalisation' is not added on to the theory (as a set of reflections on contemporary, or even historical, developments) but is built into it from the beginning, which helps explain both the strength and weakness of the theory. Luhmann has recently argued that sociology should not let geography determine its object; consequently, he rejects the determination of its object by the concept of the national state (Luhmann, 1992a:68). More radically, Luhmann even argues that only animal societies let space determine their boundaries, whereas human societies use language, writing and telecommunication for such purposes (ibid.:73). Because the social system works communicatively, its limits must be the limits of human communication. Only in modernity, however, is this limit reached. Hence Luhmann conceptualises modern society as world society that emerges at the beginning of modernity with the breakthrough from stratification to functional differentiation. The existence of world society, however, has not produced a world political system, which for Luhmann is the only element of the modern arrangement that still submits to a principle of 'regional differentiation' (Luhmann, 1991:115). By contrast the economy is a world economy, science a world scientific system, and so on. The emergence of world society means that the focus of evolution shifts from the varieties of political systems (and the selection of variants out of this diversity) to the differentiated functional sub-systems themselves. As a result, evolution can now take place only at this level: evolution at the level of world society is no longer possible, for there are no alternatives to modern world society. In this respect Luhmann views the division of the world this century into capitalist and socialist blocs as a mirage that, nevertheless, enabled an already *de facto* world society its last chance to experiment with alternatives (Luhmann, 1982:342). With the end of this mirage, a plurality of possible worlds has become inconceivable. The world-wide communicative system constitutes one world that includes all possibilities (Luhmann, 1990a:178). Yet the reason that there is no world political society to match an already existent world society remains a problem that Luhmann never satisfactorily resolves. In his early work he argues that the territorial differentiation of political systems was necessary if democratic decision-making were to be possible (1982:244). Later he simply asserts that this is the best way for the political system to optimise its functioning (Luhmann, 1990a:178). More recently he has referred to this state as 'provisionally indispensable' (Luhmann, 1991:115). This is because Luhmann thinks that a democratic world state is im-probable, in so far as the participation of everybody in decision-making is difficult to envisage. This insoluble problem is translated, therefore, into the solvable problem of the prevention of war, together with the retention of territorially-defined regional political systems. The problem then becomes one of 'narrowing the danger of war through heightening the risk of war' (ibid.). Luhmann's various solutions to the problems that the theory itself sets up— namely the non-existence of a world political society corresponding to world society and hence the empirical emergence of postnational political structures—mean that their significance goes unrecognised. Luhmann's theory is, from the beginning, already too global to comprehend the phenomenon of globalisation.

Critical confrontations

Within social theory the crucial first decision is to develop either a systems-theoretical or an action-theoretical approach. That decision divides Luhmann and the later work of Parsons from theorists as different as Giddens and Bourdieu. Although 'syncretic' positions (combining elements of systems-theory and action-theory) are possible, those who occupy them reveal more often than not an underlying preference for one position or the other. I would like to approach this question, however, from the narrower vantage point of the effects of theory-choice on a theory of reflexivity. Habermas's *Knowledge and Human Interests* (1971) is a typical attempt to construct a theory of reflexivity as self-reflexivity, where the self concerned may be either an individual or a collectivity. Although the task of a critical social science of action is to break through the power blockages that hinder self-reflection, the goal of autonomy as the endpoint of self-reflection is, for Habermas, an *a priori* embedded in language. Hence the action-theoretical perspective on self-reflection is secured only by a theory of language that smuggles in particular philosophical positions from the German idealist tradition. Giddens's work on the theory of action also tries to develop a theory of reflexivity (although one that is immune to the attractions of the German idealist tradition) by taking up some elements of the Wittgensteinian tradition (Giddens, 1984). For Giddens, reflexivity is a property neither of language nor of systems but of agency. As such, it is a property of everyday action, in so far as all actors routinely monitor their own and other people's actions. This monitoring does not entail that lucidity assumed in the early Habermasian notion of self-reflection, since it operates at the level of practical (as opposed to discursive) consciousness. Although these arguments concerning reflection are totally opposed to one another—since one presupposes the highest possible level of discursivity, while the other excludes it—they both assume that reflexivity is a property of the actor rather than of the system.

Luhmann breaks with this assumption. For him, reflection or reflexivity is reconceptualised as self-reference, and as such it is a property of a system, and not of human consciousness or the subject (Luhmann, 1985a:58). Systems operate self-referentially, in so far as they use descriptions of themselves in order to monitor their own operations: in this respect they are *observing systems* (von Foerster, 1963). The theorist who observes *observing systems* produces second-order observations, and the plurality of these precludes all ideas of a privileged act of critical self-reflection. Social systems function self-referentially, according to Luhmann, in so far as they use communications to reproduce themselves (this distinguishes them from psychical systems that use consciousness). This leads to two implications: the first is a distinction between internal events (such as thoughts) and those societal events called communications; secondly, the distinction between the individual and society can be construed as a distinction between two radically different systems (Luhmann, 1992a:74–5). To put this insight very simply, as Luhmann once did: 'you cannot think my thoughts, but you can read my communications'. This way of constructing the problem of self-reference is explicitly antihumanist, because the human being is constructed by Luhmann as an amalgam of living and conscious systems. In Luhmann's formulation, 'there is no autopoietic unity of all the autopoietic systems that compose the human being' (Luhmann, 1990a:117); or, more succinctly, 'man is not a system' (Luhmann, 1985a:68). This critique of consciousness— which stresses communication and difference rather than the unity of the individual and consciousness—uncannily parallels, as I will show later, the strategy of deconstruction. Luhmann, of course, is well aware of this fact.

The links between functionalism and evolutionism have been such that the demise of the former has entailed a discrediting of the latter. The problem here is that the kind of evolutionism discredited is neither the current form of the theory in general nor Luhmann's development of it in particular. For Michael Mann, there is no such thing as 'a' social system, because societies are not unitary; if this is so, there can be no evolutionary development (Mann, 1986:1). There is nothing wrong with this argument, and Luhmann would agree with it, except for the proviso that a 'decentred society' differentiated into sub-systems may be describable in evolutionary terms if handled properly. Giddens's strictures against evolutionism, which are more developed than Mann's, are similarly both correct and beside the point. Although Giddens's attacks on the vacuous-ness, speciousness and developmentalism of the concept of adaptation are quite correct, they rely nevertheless on mainly nineteenth-century versions of such theories to establish their point (Giddens, 1984:233). The autopoietic turn in systems-theory results in a reworking of evolutionary theory that immunises it against these fashionable critiques. First, as we have seen, Luhmann argues that evolution no longer takes place at the level of the system as a whole, because it constitutes a unity that includes (rather than excludes) difference. Hence, evolution occurs in the sub-systems of a decentred society by means of function-specific evolutionary mechanisms, rather than through the processes of social evolution. Second, Luhmann specifically rejects the notion of adaptation as the mechanism of social evolution. Self-referential autopoietic systems demarcate themselves from an environment with which they do not interchange, and which may disturb or irritate them in the process of their own internal reproduction and development. Conceived of in this way, the system 'is not forced to adapt by the environment nor allowed to reproduce only through the best possible adaptation' (Luhmann, 1989:13). Or, an even more radical formulation: 'The system not only does not adapt itself to its environment, but chooses or alters the environment in order to adapt it to what the system itself prefers' (Luhmann, 1990b:552). Third, Luhmann's notion of social evolution involves no periodisa-tion of history but tries to analyse structural changes merely through the use of the terms 'variation', 'selection' and 'stabilisation'. Although the conceptualisation of those three types of differentiation may suggest such a phase-theory (in so far as it separates archaic and traditional from modern societies), the stabilisation of selected variants is always presented by Luhmann as a contingent and episodic shift, rather than as a lawful and developmental process. Hence Luhmann manages to reconceptualise change in a way that is remarkably similar not only to Mann's notions of 'overlapping networks' and 'leading edges' but also to Giddens's notions of 'episodes' and 'time-space wedges'. He manages to do so, however, from within (rather than from outside) a reformulated evolutionary theory.

The debate between Luhmann and Habermas is both long standing and multifaceted. In the early 1970s Habermas criticised Luhmann's theory for being the highest expression of 'technocratic consciousness'. Luhmann replied by accusing Habermas of 'a scientifically immanent politicisation' of his theory, which rested on the distinction between critical and apologetic theories of social domination (Habermas, 1971:145, 399). Luhmann showed how critical and apologetic theories 'tumble over into one another', and severed the Habermasian link between reason and freedom from domination. In the mid 1980s the debate re-emerged with re-workings of both Habermas's and Luhmann's theories. Although this renewed debate has not been as direct and thorough as the first, the main elements of discord are clearly discernible. I would like to focus on the debate in so far as it concerns the problem of reason, both in philosophical and sociological terms. Habermas conceptualised the reworking of his theory as an attempt to go beyond a solipsistic philosophy of consciousness and toward a linguistically founded philosophy of intersubjectivity. When Habermas criticises Luhmann's theory for being not so much sociology as an appropriation of the philosophy of consciousness, he associates it therefore with an out-moded philosophy. Habermas further argues that the system–intersubjectivity problem is merely an updated version of the mind–body problem (that is, the problem that separates monological from communicationally orientated theories). According to Habermas, the systems-theoretical concept of rationality shrinks reason to the reduction of complexity, and Luhmann's concept of society denies it the possibility of obtaining a rational identity (Habermas, 1987). Luhmann's response to the first argument is to deny that the Enlightenment concept of reason (to which Habermas is still committed) continues to be valid when opposed by a radically constructivist notion of rationality. For Luhmann, there are two forms of observation. 'First-order observation' involves the observation of objects which, instead of being pre-given, are themselves empirical constructions created by observing with distinctions. 'Second-order observation' involves observing those observations, which involves observing those distinctions used (but not taken notice of) by first-order observation. Second-order observation is for Luhmann a matter of reflection or rationality rather than of reason, for it results in no unitary description of the world. However, second-order observation itself uses distinctions, and these also presuppose blind spots not observable from within the distinctions themselves. We begin with a difference and end with a difference, and both the distinction we choose to begin with, and the distinction with which we choose to observe this distinction, could have been different. The contingency of our distinctions, and the possibility of their substitution, are presumed in Luhmann's account of rationality. From Luhmann's standpoint, this is not the case with Habermas's discourse theory and its consensus theory of truth. Rational consensus, according to Luhmann, is 'a boundary case of extreme improbability', and he argues that the introduction of such a description into society produces difference and not unity (Luhmann, 1987:45, 49). Luhmann's response to the second argument runs parallel to his first. Just as observation works with difference, so also do the sub-systems of modern society. For Luhmann, because society does not constitute a totality, a rational identity is not something to which it could aim. Society is difference: a multiplicity of different sub-systems, which themselves function only through difference. Society does not and could not conform to reason, because its decentred space is contingent and open to the possibility of substitution. Significantly, however, Luhmann thinks these possibilities of substitution are limited, and sees change as a 'catastrophe', that is, as an 'abrupt transition to another form of stability' (Luhmann, 1992b:48). What this terminology deliberately excludes are those Enlightenment projects for social change that still linger in attempts at constructing a more rational identity for modern society. There is no position outside of society from which one could observe the difference between rationality and irrationality and then use it in order to make a global judgement. Furthermore, the focus on identity as such fails to recognise that society exists only as contingent difference.

Luhmann's critique of Habermas brings systems-theory into close connection with postmodernism in general and Derrida in particular. As there is no external observer, there can be no meta-narrative; in so far as there is no meta-narrative, Luhmann sees some validity in postmodernism. For Luhmann, however, this is neither a post-Auschwitz nor even a contemporary development, but something which emerges with the advent of modernity itself. In other words, Luhmann redescribes postmodernism as a belated recognition of the contingency of modernity. If there is no external observer, then all observation takes place only within the system. For Luhmann, the observer within the system is in the position of the devil, observing the observations of God—which is a position that theologians also occupied, and with which they felt distinctly uncomfortable (Luhmann, 1992b:109–10). Luhmann sees deconstruction as also one-sidedly occupying this position. He demonstrates this by translating Derrida's philosophy of *deconstruction* into Günther's notion of 'polycontexturality', since 'all determinations only make sense when they occur in the context of a distinction' (Luhmann, 1990c:78). Deconstruction, therefore, is second-order observation that deconstructs those first-order distinctions which are necessarily blind both to the kind of distinction they use and the context out of which they emerge. Yet Luhmann sees deconstruction as (like postmodernism) a belated recognition of the contingency of an old European cognitive apparatus (with its repertoire of distinctions) rather than as a theory capable of accounting for modern society. As Luhmann puts it, because a 'semantic *catastrophe*' separates premodernity from modernity, the means of deconstruction must be chosen not merely with a view to deconstructing that metaphysical tradition we have lost, but also with a view to describing the '*postcatastrophical* condition' we have inherited (Luhmann, 1993:777). Whatever one thinks of Luhmann's proposals, this judgement of Derrida's social theory as an incoherent mixture of Heidegger and Marx is hard to fault.

Conclusion

Luhmann is a lover of paradox, and places it (rather than parody) at the centre of cognition. It should come as no surprise, therefore, that Luhmann's paradoxical achievement is to have created a theory of modernity that does not remain immune to postmodernism but, on the contrary, has theorised its insights in advance through the radical reworking of the theory of modernity itself. The paradoxical achievement of Luhmann's work could not (and does not) end there, however, but recurs endlessly. As a theory it posits that the unity of society consists in its multiplicity, and therefore that the theory of society itself can be never more than a multiplicity of second-order observations. It suggests that we are moving toward a world society which is not a world political system, because its unity lies in the multiplicity of those functional sub-systems of which it consists. In such a world, moreover, a multiplicity of theories will thrive (rather than be extinguished) through its further unification. Hence for Luhmann 'a polycontextural world' does not admit of any binding representation by himself or anybody else (Luhmann, 1992b:84–5). Post-metaphysical thought is founded, therefore, not on the proceduralisation of reason, but on 'emancipation from reason': *Nie wieder Vernunft* (Never again reason) (ibid.:76). Rather than pursuing a philosophy of *deconstruction* (that would merely deconstruct those differences that metaphysical thought used but could not observe), Luhmann constructs a theory of difference on which to base not only a theory of theory but also a theory of society. Unlike both utopian projections of unity and deconstructions of metaphysical distinctions, Luhmann's theory evinces neither the progressive optimism of the former nor the radical chic of the latter. Luhmann envisages a society that works well but could just as easily not have come into existence, and might equally endanger its own existence. This contingent and differentialist picture of societal functioning is constructed with a diabolical scepticism that only an observer within the system could make credible.

5

From Text to System: Recent German Literary Theory

David Roberts

Up to the 1960s literary theory in Germany was dominated by the nineteenth-century tradition of philosophical hermeneutics, reflected in the concentration on an exclusive canon of classical texts, which functioned to insulate the study of literature from the realities of social and literary change. More particularly, the restriction of West German scholarship after 1945 to the New Criticism's programme of immanent analysis served to repress the Nazi past of the discipline and the propagandistic perversion of literary history and criticism during the Third Reich. The defensive hegemony of this purely 'literary' self-understanding disintegrated in the 1960s in the face of challenges from a politically engaged student generation, determined to unmask the political and moral evasions of its fathers and to revolutionise the study of literature by turning to Marxist, ideological-critical and psychoanalytic theories. The influence of linguistics, structuralism and various poststructuralisms has been less pronounced. French theory, unlike its reception in the Anglo-American world, has been vigorously contested (most notably: Jürgen Habermas, 1987) in the context of debates in the 1980s on modernism and postmodernism.

In the field of literary theory the search in the 1960s for new orientations and paradigms resulted, on the one hand, in the renewal of hermeneutics in the form of reception theory, and on the other in the rediscovery and reappropriation of Marxism and the critical theory of the Frankfurt School, whose political and ideological-

critical focus was transformed in the 1970s into competing programmes for a social history of German literature. Methodological
difficulties, posed by the problem of defining the connections between the literary and the social spheres without falling back into
orthodox Marxism's economic and class determination, led in the
1980s to a growing interest in Niklas Luhmann's systems-theory of
society, which appears to offer a more adequate conceptual framework for analysing literature as a social sphere in its own right.

The 1960s was the decisive period of reorientation. My starting
point, however, is two works of the older generation which frame
this decade, Hans-Georg Gadamer's *Truth and Method* (1960) and
Theodor Adorno's *Aesthetic Theory* (1970). Gadamer follows Martin
Heidegger's renewal of that tradition of hermeneutic theory which
goes back to German Romanticism; Adorno stands in the tradition
of a Hegelian–Marxian philosophy of history. What both have in
common is the privileging of the work of art as a form of truth in
opposition to the dominance of scientific method in the modern
world. Moreover, for both Gadamer and Adorno understanding
and interpretation are dependent on historical awareness. The
linking of past and present in that fusion of horizons of which
Gadamer speaks is realised in our present (i.e. historically situated)
understanding of the past. Understanding is the process by which
tradition is appropriated in and for the present. Similarly, according
to Adorno, the significance and truth of works of art are accessible
only to a historical consciousness which is able to read in the work
of art the signs of the times. What these signs reveal is the inexorable
progress of economic, scientific and social rationalisation, which
threatens the very possibility of human experience and artistic
creation. Thus, if for Gadamer historical consciousness is the
condition of the continuity of tradition, its message for Adorno is
the crisis of tradition, whose corollary is an aesthetics of negativity.
The crisis of social progress confronts modern art with a self-
destructive paradox: only by destroying tradition can the authentic
work of art remain faithful to tradition. The vanishing point of
Adorno's aesthetics are Samuel Beckett's variations on the 'endgame'
of history and progress.

Gadamer and Adorno provide the immediate points of departure
for the two main lines of German literary theory which have entered

the international scene since the 1970s: the Constance school of
reception aesthetics (Hans Robert Jauss and Wolfgang Iser), and
analyses of the institution of literature by Peter and Christa Bürger.

Reader reception theory

Jauss was a pupil of Gadamer. His original project of revitalising
the writing of literary history may be characterised as the attempt
to combine Russian and Prague Formalism with Gadamer's hermeneutics. It aimed to bridge the gap between literary and general
history, between text and context, by means of a history of the
reception of texts. The difficulties involved led to a modification
which brought out more clearly Jauss's underlying interest. The
history of reception was transformed into an enquiry into aesthetic
experience, which embraced not only the production and reception of texts but also the social (i.e. communicative) function of
literature.

In his inaugural lecture of 1967 at the University of Constance,
'Literary History as a Challenge to Literary Theory' (Jauss, 1982b),
Jauss defined literary history as a 'process of aesthetic reception
and production which takes place in the realisation of literary texts'
by readers, critics and authors. In other words, literary history must
break with the one-sided concentration on works and authors (the
paradigm of production) familiar from traditional literary histories
but also evident in Marxist and Formalist approaches. Neither the
Marxist emphasis on the social determinants of literary production
nor the Formalist emphasis on such autonomous mechanisms in
the evolution of the 'literary series' as the innovative estrangement
of canonised genres and conventions leaves room for a recognition of either the role of the reader or the 'effective history'
(Gadamer) of literary texts. According to Jauss, the concentration
on production severs the links between past and present because
it ignores the fact that literary history is a process constituted by the
dialogical relation of question and answer between works and
readers, including their authors. In order to reconstruct this process,
Jauss takes a couple of features from Formalism—the understanding of literature as a system of genres, and of literary history as a
changing succession of genre systems—and embeds them in

Gadamer's horizon of understanding. By combining the Formalist dynamic of literary innovation with the hermeneutic horizon of readers' expectations, Jauss can argue that the 'literary series' is to be viewed as an ongoing formulation and reformulation of problems and solutions, constituted by the dialogic interaction between reception and production. Literary hermeneutics, Jauss writes, undertakes

> the task of interpreting the tension between text and the present as a process in which the dialogue between author, reader, and a new author deals with the temporal distance in the back-and-forth of question and answer, of original answer, present question, and new solution, and concretizes meaning in ever different ways, and therefore more richly. (Jauss, 1982a:xxxvi).

Given that the history of literary production is realised in a history of reception which reconnects past and present, Jauss sees reception as the means by which literary historians can define the original significance of texts and trace the history of changing evaluations as witnessed in their canonisation, marginalisation, and reappropriation. Jauss claims that his model solves a perennial problem of literary history, namely how the 'literary series' is to be related to what he calls the general process of history. His proposed mediation between the literary and the historical dimensions of literary history amounts, however, only to a more sophisticated history of the literary system itself, which foregrounds the role of reception. That is to say, the historical dimension of literary history is observable not in the effect of society on literature but in the effect of literature on society. Individual works can alter the perceptions of readers by challenging their horizon of expectations, which is constituted not only by aesthetic but also by social norms. Literature thus has a 'socially formative function'.

This turn to the social function of literature remains undeveloped in 'Literary History as a Challenge to Literary Theory'. It occupies, however, a central place in his subsequent work, which was triggered by his response to the publication of Adorno's *Aesthetic Theory*. Adorno's 'aesthetics of negativity' led Jauss to reconsider his reliance on the Formalist conception of literary evolution predicated on the negation of existing literary models. The key concept which now emerges is 'aesthetic experience', which Jauss opposes to the aesthetics of negativity that characterised the modernist and avant-garde programmes of the Formalists and Adorno. Jauss rejects Adorno's pessimistic diagnosis of the situation of art in capitalist society, which allows only the extremes of total conformity or total nonconformity. If for Adorno authentic art preserves its critical function by means of negativity, the culture industry by contrast reduces the social function of art to a celebration of the relentless functioning of the market, for which the artwork is simply a commodity. The alternatives are an elitist and avant-garde aesthetics of negativity or the affirmative culture of mass entertainment. According to Jauss the consequences for aesthetic experience are two versions of the denial of aesthetic pleasure: the avant-garde's suspicion of pleasure as complicit with the market is complemented by the culture industry's degradation of pleasure to manipulated consumption. If the premodern formula for the social function of art was the combination of instruction with pleasure, Adorno's diagnosis reveals their divorce in a capitalist market economy: instruction-without-pleasure or pleasure-without-instruction are the sundered halves of a lost unity. Jauss questions this separation of the truth-content of works of art from aesthetic pleasure. Adorno's aesthetics of negativity is for him only the latest and most extreme example of the priority accorded to the truth of art in aesthetic theory and the privileging of production over reception. Thus in his defence of aesthetic experience Jauss reworks the old formula of instruction and pleasure: 'The primary experience of a work of art takes place in the orientation to its aesthetic effect, in an understanding which is pleasure, and a pleasure which is cognitive' (Jauss, 1982a:xxix). The restoration of the lost unity involves a double distancing from Adorno. On the one hand, Adorno's theory applies only to modern art. On the other, the binary schema of negation/affirmation does not account for the communicative function of art. Jauss insists that aesthetic production and reception cannot be equated solely with economic production and consumption: the work of art is not a commodity, and aesthetic experience implies a freedom which exceeds manipulation.

Jauss's revision of his original project of a reception-based literary history is summed up by the title of his book, *Aesthetic Experience and Literary Hermeneutics*. Jauss presents his defence of aesthetic pleasure in the major essay, 'A Sketch of a Theory and History of Aesthetic Experience', in terms of the affinity between aesthetic experience and the attitude we adopt towards play. Playful simulation involves both participation and distance, identification and detachment. In the experience of a work of art we distance ourselves from our everyday attitudes in order to participate freely in an imaginary world. This free participation is the source of pleasure that arises from the dialogue between reader and text, and requires the 'imagining, testing and meaning-creating activity' of the reader. The dialogue between reader and text thus involves a constant interplay between two poles: surrender to aesthetic effect, and critical distance from the text. The experience of a second world disclosed by the text is an experience of the self as self and as other. This hermeneutic merging of horizons does not obliterate the difference between self and other, for if it did it would destroy the very condition of aesthetic experience, the freedom of participation. The realisation of the text in the act of reception and understanding rests on the pleasurable tension of this difference. As Jauss expresses it: 'Aesthetic experience that thus occurs in a state of balance between disinterested contemplation and testing participation is a mode of experiencing oneself in a possible being other which the aesthetic mode opens up' (Jauss, 1982a:32).

The form of aesthetic experience with which we are most familiar is reception. For Jauss reception is only one of the three dimensions of aesthetic experience, which is central because it mediates between production on the one side and intersubjective communication on the other. Jauss terms these three dimensions *poiesis, aisthesis* and *catharsis*. They are the three functions of the attitude of aesthetic enjoyment which frees us both *from* and *for* something:

> for the producing consciousness, in the production of the world as its own work (poiesis); for the receiving consciousness, in the seizing of the possibility of renewing one's perception of outer and inner reality (aisthesis), and finally—and here subjective opens up toward intersubjective experience—in the assent to a judgement demanded by the work, or in the identification with

sketched and further-to-be-defined norms of action [catharsis]. (ibid.:35)

As the quotation makes clear, it is through the third function that the experience of art achieves its socially formative effect. Just as reception entails a testing participation, so in turn individual reception must test its judgement in the dialogue with other recipients. All judgements must appeal to norms, and norms are the result of intersubjective consensus which can be attained only through freely given assent. Jauss's model for aesthetic judgement is taken from Kant's *Critique of Judgement*, but it is also close to Habermas's ideal of domination-free discourse. Jauss's return to Kant distinguishes the Constance school from those aesthetic theories (deriving from Hegel) in which the work of art is understood as the revelation of truth, whether it be the revelation of the negative truth of our socio-historical condition (Adorno) or the truth of Being (Heidegger). Instead of concentrating on an aesthetics of production, the Constance school emphasises the free co-creative function of reception. The work of art accordingly is the sum of its cumulatively enriched reception. If the original intention of constructing literary history as the sum of such 'effective histories' was clearly unmanageable, the horizon of literary history is retained in the dialogic structure which underpins aesthetic experience. The social function of art is vindicated within the Enlightenment tradition of dialogic communication, in which aesthetic production, reception and judgement form a continuum that connects art and life. We find in the work of Wolfgang Iser a similar trajectory from the text (understood as a communicative structure to be realised by the reader) to those human needs to which literature responds. This trajectory is described by the title of his recent collection of essays: *Prospecting: From Reader Response to Literary Anthropology* (1989).

Iser first became known through the publication of *The Implied Reader: Patterns of Communication in Prose Fiction from Bunyan to Beckett* (1974). In his essay on aesthetic experience Jauss writes: 'the world appears as the horizon of fiction, fiction appears as the horizon of the world' (Jauss, 1982a:122). Iser gives a similar definition of the function of the novel, which is to involve readers in the world of the novel and so help them to understand it and thereby their own world more clearly. The encounter between individual readers and the text produces the 'implied reader': 'The term incorporates both the restructuring of the potential meaning by the text, and the reader's actualization of this potential through the reading process' (Iser, 1974:xii). Historically Iser observes a progressive emancipation of the implied reader. If the eighteenth-century novel's inquiry into human nature and the principles of moral conduct was effected through direct guidance of the reader, the presentation of the complexities of subjectivity in the nineteenth-century novel called for indirect guidance of the reader. The self-reflexive novels of the twentieth century pose in turn the question of meaning and identity by denying the reader's expectations of meaning and coherence. Readers are forced to examine their own unreflected interpretations of the world through the fictional frustration of interpretation. It is against this historical background that Iser constructs in the final chapter his phenomenological account of the 'reading process'. As we have seen, the implied reader is the joint outcome of production and reception, of artistic realisation (the text) and aesthetic realisation (the reader). The implied reader thus signifies the merging of horizons effected by the concretisation of the virtual meaning of the text in the reading process. To the extent that the fictional text does not confirm the reader's expectations, a dialogic learning process is set in motion in which every reader is constructed by the text at the same time as he or she constructs it. Historically this can be traced as a process which takes us from the implied reader as a function of the text in the eighteenth century to the text as a function of interpretation in the twentieth century, a process which explains in turn the emergence of reception theory. The emancipation of the reader goes hand in hand with the growing indeterminacy of the text, which Iser considers in two essays: 'Indeterminacy and the Reader's Response in Prose Fiction' and 'Interaction between Text and Reader' (Iser, 1989). These take up the themes of his second book, *The Act of Reading: A Theory of Aesthetic Response* (1978).

Iser argues that indeterminacy is the means by which the reader is both incorporated in the text and the key to the interaction, in which text and reader control and regulate each other. The activating trigger of reader response is given by textual gaps or blanks, which function as the open, suspended connections between explicit and implicit meaning, the manifest and latent dimensions of the text. Behind the readable text lies the unreadable text. This helps us to understand why the world and fiction are each other's horizon. If we take the world as the horizon of fiction, then the indeterminacy of the text simulates the open and unfinalisable nature of our experience of the world. This is why the novel works directly or indirectly with a plurality of viewpoints, since its most general theme is the tension between the readable and unreadable text of society and human behaviour. Reading involves the negotiation of this interplay between coherence and incoherence, between the fiction's illusion of the real and its negation of illusion. When this interplay points beyond the observation of society to the question of observation itself, then what results is the self-observing, self-reflexive novel. Now fiction becomes the horizon of the world, and the act of reading becomes the model of world interpretation. And this is what Iser means when he terms his analysis of the reading process 'phenomenological'. The reader's constitution of the text is analogous to the process by which we constitute the world.

In his essay on 'Changing Functions of Literature' (Iser, 1989), Iser takes issue with the ideological-critical assertion that literature in bourgeois society has an affirmative function (Marcuse, Bürger) which can be countered only by an avant-gardist aesthetics of negativity (Adorno). Iser (like Jauss) rejects this exclusive and reductive alternative, which fails to grasp that the ultimate dimension of aesthetic experience is imaginary. Literature 'reveals the vast number of ways in which human faculties can be used to open up the world in which we live'. Reading is in both senses of the word an imaginary training in interpretation: 'What makes literature so fascinating and relevant today is the discovery that all our activities are permeated by acts of interpretation—indeed, that we live *by* interpretation' (Iser, 1989:209). Thus in 'Toward a Literary Anthropology' Iser asks why we need fiction, and answers with Nelson Goodman: 'Fictions are ways of worldmaking' (ibid.:270). While worldmaking is undoubtedly an anthropological constant of all human societies, to see such worldmaking as fictional is a specifically modern perspective. Iser's literary anthropology is directed to the capacity of modern fiction to deepen our awareness of the inner world of the self, and to open up social alternatives by going beyond and transforming the given world of experience. This activation of the reader's imaginative resources in the co-creation of possible worlds is indeed central to modern as opposed to premodern literature. Correspondingly, the modern problem of interpretation arises once literature is no longer understood as the imitation of nature. The outcome, to put it paradoxically, is the 'fictionalization' of literature. The old doctrine of the congruence between art and nature gives way by the eighteenth century to an understanding of literature as an interplay between fiction and reality, possible and given worlds, in which the reader is accorded an ever more important synthesising role. That is why Jauss places aesthetic experience—and Iser the act of reading—at the centre of literary theory. The deficiency in Iser's approach lies in his neglect of the intersubjective dimension of reception. The social communicative function of literature is confined to the interaction between reader and text. It does not include the public dimension of aesthetic judgement (Jauss) or deal with the question of the 'interpretative community' (Fish, 1980), which incorporates the already given conventions of interpretation. Equally, for all his justified criticism of the ideological-critical approach, Iser's phenomenological approach does not allow him to deal adequately with the historical dimension of these conventions, which are the focus of Peter and Christa Bürger's work.

The institution of literature

Peter Bürger is best known for his *Theory of the Avant-Garde*, first published in 1974 (Bürger, 1984). In this short but influential study, he sets out to define the present situation of art and the tasks of a critical literary theory. *The Theory of the Avant-Garde* appeared four years after Adorno's *Aesthetic Theory*. This proximity only underlines, however, the radical historical break between the generations, brought into the open by the student revolt in Germany and the events of May 1968 in Paris. The combination of political revolt and surrealist happening in May 1968 seemed to suggest a

renewal of the avant-garde impulses of the 1920s. The dissipation
of these dreams of political and cultural revolution forms the
background to Bürger's diagnosis of the present situation of art. In
brief his argument is this: the driving force of the historical avant-
garde movements at the end of World War I (Dada, Surrealism,
Russian Constructivism) was the desire to overcome the gulf
between art and life through the total challenge to what Bürger
calls the bourgeois institution of art. The failure of the avant-garde's
challenge has critical consequences for both art and art theory. To
understand these consequences we must first clarify what constitutes
the historical significance of the avant-garde's challenge and its
failure.

For Bürger the avant-garde movements of the first two decades
of this century are not just another stage or episode in the history
of modern art since the eighteenth century. On the contrary they
represent a unique vantage point from which the developmental
tendencies of art in bourgeois society can be grasped and reconstructed. To put the argument the other way round: the avant-
garde challenge to the bourgeois institution of art can occur only
when the inherent tendencies of bourgeois art have been fully
revealed. These tendencies lie for Bürger in the progressive
elimination of the political content of art-works in favour of
questions of form and style, which finds its fullest expression in the
aestheticism of the late nineteenth century with its doctrine of art
for art's sake. The avant-garde revolt against the separation of art
and life is not to be understood as a strategy for continuing
bourgeois art by other means, but as the expression of a total
break with tradition. It is this will to achieve a total break which
makes the avant-garde the *self-critique* of art in bourgeois society.
The revolutionary aims of avant-garde movements are thus both
political and critical, and, since the *political* dream of the utopian
fusion of art and life necessarily failed, the *critical* legacy is all the
more significant. If the avant-garde challenge lays bare (estranges)
the bourgeois institution of art, the failure of the challenge reveals
that the condition of post-avant-garde art is one in which the political
content of art-works and the possibility of revolutionary change
are neutralised by the institution. If this is the case, what are the
consequences for a critical theory of art? Bürger's argument is

directed against the aesthetic theory of Adorno, which is resolutely modernist in its insistence on the inescapable force of artistic innovation and rationalisation. But if the possibility of artistic progress collapses with the failure of the avant-garde, where does this leave Adorno's avant-gardist aesthetics? Just as importantly, and here the influence of Herbert Marcuse becomes apparent, Bürger's *Theory of the Avant-Garde* is directed against Adorno's insistence on the *autonomy* of modern art and his hostility to all forms and programmes of 'engaged' art. Adorno's privileging of innovation and autonomy reveals his underlying affinity with the bourgeois institution of art. If critical theory is to be truly critical it must turn its own critical weapons against itself.

Two steps are involved: the first is the appropriation of Marcuse's seminal essay of 1937, 'The Affirmative Character of Culture' (Marcuse, 1968), together with his *Essay on Liberation* (1969)—written in response to the rise of the New Left in the USA and in Europe—in which Marcuse calls for the reunion of art and life. The 1937 essay takes up Marx's critique of religion and applies it to the situation of art in bourgeois society, which permits the expression of emancipatory human values only in fictional form, thereby hindering an understanding of the connection between the practical (political) ineffectivity of art and its autonomous status. Marcuse's critique of the affirmative character of art provides Bürger with the basis for his concept of the bourgeois institution of art, which determines the conditions in which works of art are produced and received in capitalist society.

The second step is more radical. By making progress (innovation) the key to his aesthetic theory, Adorno foregrounds the connection between the history and the theory of modern art. If, however, aesthetic theory is itself a historical product, then it too must be historicised in order to uncover the historical limits of its application. Adorno's *Aesthetic Theory*, as seen from the vantage point of Bürger's *Theory of the Avant-Garde*, is a theory which has failed to grasp the historical significance of the failure of the avant-garde. Adorno's categories, especially the category of progress, no longer apply to the post-avant-garde situation of art. The historical limits of Adorno's theory signify for Bürger the crisis of the whole tradition of neo-Marxist aesthetic theory, inspired by the Hegelian combination of philosophy of history and philosophy of art. In its place Bürger proposes the programme of a 'critical literary theory', whose outline he sketches in the Introduction to *Theory of the Avant-Garde*.

Literary theory for Bürger is critical in so far as it subjects its own activities and categories to scrutiny. It thus stands apart from and outside the affirmative stance of traditional literary theory which is incapable of critical self-examination (i.e. incapable of asking what theoretical questions its categories permit and exclude). Bürger allies himself with Habermas's critique of Gadamer's conservative understanding of hermeneutics (Habermas, 1988). Instead of the power of 'prejudice' (pre-understanding) for the interpreting of tradition, Bürger pleads for the critical 'power of reflection', whose task is to criticise the ideology enshrined in the institution of litera- ture and its norms of production and reception. Bürger conceives of his critical literary theory as the ideology-critical successor to the bourgeois aesthetics of autonomy. This includes both Adorno and Lukács, since neither questions such basic normative categories of bourgeois aesthetics as the primacy of production over reception (the artist as genius), the organic work of art, the concept of progress (aesthetic innovation), and so on. These normative categories are to be replaced by an ideological-critical investigation into the social function of art, that is, the contradictory relation between cultural products and social conditions. By switching attention from the autonomous work of art to the doctrine of autonomy, Bürger is arguing that the object of critical literary theory is no longer the text itself but the institution which frames the text. Or rather, more precisely, the relation between text and institution, that Bürger formulates in the following fashion: 'The institution functions within the work, just as the work functions within the institution' (Bürger, 1992:17).

This formulation comes from his essay on 'The Institution of Art as a Category of the Sociology of Literature' in Peter and Christa Bürger's *The Institutions of Art* (Bürger and Bürger, 1992). In this essay Bürger argues that the sociology of literature must be judged on its ability to combine the critique of individual texts with an analysis of the 'structural mechanisms of influence' underlying reception. In proposing that a theory of the historical transformations of the social function of literature (i.e. the historically changing institutionalisations of literature) provides the key to the link between text and social context, Bürger is seeking a more satisfactory answer to Jauss's original project of a literary history based on reception. What makes it more satisfactory is that it does not treat text and context—in Jauss's terms, the 'literary series' and the general process of history—as two separate and independent phenomena. For Bürger both text and context are mediated by the institution of literature. It is this which allows a sociology of literature to overcome on the one hand the exclusive alternatives of a hermeneutics devoted to the text as against an empirical sociology of literature, and on the other hand to break with the orthodox Marxist account of the relation between ideological superstructure and socio-economic base, in which works of literature are to be read as revealing or obscuring the contradictions of class society. Bürger's concern is not the text as a social document but those successive institutionalisations of literature that determine the changing social functions of literature. It is precisely an awareness of these historical changes and their correlation with succeeding social formations that underlies Bürger's insistence on a historicising account of the bourgeois institution of literature. At the same time it is precisely the persistence of the bourgeois institution that has led him to confront it with its Enlightenment origins. Here is a parallel to Habermas's reconstruction of the public sphere as a historical category of bourgeois society. The structural transformation of the public sphere from a culture-judging to a culture-consuming public, in which the literary public sphere has lost its specific character and has been replaced by the culture of the mass media, can be seen as providing the wider framework for Bürger's reconstruction of the bourgeois institution of literature as a historical category. The two crucial moments in the history of the institution are the period around 1800, in which the Enlightenment model is displaced by the Romantic, and the second decade of this century, when the avant-garde challenge lays bare the limits of the institution.

The challenge of Peter and Christa Bürger's work to the bourgeois institution of literary theory and criticism is brought out clearly in Russell A. Berman's introduction to *The Institutions of Art*. Despite all the debates on literary theory in the USA from reader reception to deconstruction, Berman maintains that the core of the discipline still remains close reading based on the hermeneutics of the individual text. Reader-reception and reader-response theory may well have discredited the assumption of a stable textual meaning and replaced it with the plurality of interpretations which reflect the co-constitution of the text by the reader. Nevertheless, the 'authority of interpretative communities' (i.e. the hermeneutic model) is not itself questioned, whether it is based on the assumption of the informed reader or, as with deconstruction, on the authority of the critic. The hermeneutic model privileges, as Berman puts it, a specific 'preunderstanding' of literature. This derives from the Romantic aesthetics of autonomy, which challenged and replaced the Enlightenment's moral-didactic enlistment of literature in the cause of progress, a move which in turn had challenged and displaced the feudal-absolutist conception of art as serving the self-representation and glorification of the court and the nobility. If the Enlightenment conception of the function of art was directed one-sidedly to the goal of social emancipation, the Romantic response was to affirm just as one-sidedly the emancipation of art from social constraints and functions. The result was a corresponding marginalisation of social and political issues that is still evident in literary criticism and theory today.

The thrust of Bürger's call for a critical literary theory lies in the importance attached to the question of the social function of art in bourgeois-capitalist society. As we have seen, Jauss rejects Adorno's exclusive alternative of an affirmative culture industry and an avant-gardist aesthetics of negativity to insist with Iser on the 'imaginary, testing and meaning-creating activity' of aesthetic experience. However, from the perspective of reader reception, which foregrounds the freedom of the reader, Bürger's account of the norms governing production and reception must appear too reductive. There is also a more fundamental objection to Bürger's sociology of literature, an objection which is itself sociological. Bürger's critique of the doctrine of autonomy reads in Marxist fashion the separation of literature from life as a process of alienation. Artistic freedom is achieved at the price of its social and political impotence. If, however, we read the separation of literature and life not as the historical reflection of the experience of social alienation (Bürger and Bürger, 1992:7) but as a result of the functional differentiation of modern society (which leads to the emergence of autonomous social sub-systems such as politics, law, economy, education or art), then we must pose the question of the social function of art in a different way. Seen in this light, the political neutralisation of literature in bourgeois society reflects the fact that modern society possesses a functionally differentiated system devoted to politics. It is only where an autonomous political system is absent or suppressed (as for instance in the societies of state socialism) that literature takes on an eminently political role, while officially approved writing by contrast functions as a direct or indirect branch of state propaganda. In other words, the doctrine of artistic autonomy is to be construed not as a hidden confession of political impotence but as a consequence of the emergence of a literary system whose social function can be fulfilled by no other specialised sub-system of society. The problem is that Bürger's definition of the social function of art simultaneously acknowledges and denies the 'differentiation of a social subsector for art':

> This differentiated social subsector, which functions according to its own rules, still depends on the social whole, for which it undertakes particular tasks. The concept of autonomy may, for some artists, be associated with the idea of independence from society, but as we have seen in Schiller's theory, the concept functions institutionally to mean emancipation from *immediate* demands for social application; this emancipation is, however, achieved so as to enable art to perform functions for society as a whole which are not (or no longer thoroughly) performed by other institutions. Art is institutionalized as autonomous to act as guardian of human emancipation in a society whose actual life process does not allow its realisation. (Bürger and Bürger, 1992:10)

What Bürger grants with one hand he takes back with the other. Literature does indeed comprise a differentiated subsector of society; its autonomy, however, is mere appearance, since in relation to the functioning of society as a whole it serves only as the mask of social alienation. Bürger thus reverses the implications of autonomy. What is at issue is not the negative understanding of autonomy as dependence on society as a whole, but on the contrary the question of how the literary system responds to the social-structural necessity —brought about by functional differentiation—of becoming autonomous through the reflection of its identity. Bürger's ideological reading of the function of literature means that his programme of 'critical literary theory' remains tied to the nineteenth-century Marxist theory of alienation, whose explanatory power in relation to modern society is no longer evident. It is for this reason that Luhmann's systems-theory, which replaces critical theory's paradigm of alienation with the paradigm of functional differentiation, is attracting increasing attention from literary scholars in Germany. Does it offer the basis for a new paradigm in literary theory? It is too early to answer this question, as the theoretical debate has hardly begun, but in what follows I will indicate some of the main responses so far.

Systems theory

Two main lines of development by literary scholars are evident in the short history of the reception of systems theory. The one— represented by Siegfried J. Schmidt's book *Die Selbstorganisation des Sozialsystems Literatur im 18. Jahrhundert* (1989)—sets out to reconstruct the emergence of an autonomous or self-organising literary system in the second half of the eighteenth century as part of the process of the functional differentiation of society. The interest of this study, which 'systematizes' in a double sense Schmidt's earlier programme of an empirical theory of literature, lies in the constitution of literature as a social system, and accordingly in a switch from a hermeneutics of the text to a sociology of the literary system. The other line of reception—represented by Dietrich Schwanitz's book *Systemtheorie und Literatur* (1990)—takes as its perspective the self-reference of literature, which is seen as operating by means of a difference in information between the observer and the observed. Here the self-organisation of literature is defined not through the socio-historical process of functional differentiation but in terms of the emergence of self-referential observation. The two approaches are complementary, since functional differentiation is dependent upon the feedback given by what Luhmann calls 'second-order' observation. The underlying difference is nevertheless significant. Schmidt's formula for paradigm change—'from text to literary system'—is directed to a new conceptual framework for the sociology of the literary system, whereas Schwanitz's new paradigm is oriented to the evolution and differentiation of literary genres. Schwanitz is closer to Luhmann's understanding of social systems as meaning-constituting systems, constituted by self-referential communication which draws the boundary between a system and its environment. Schmidt on the other hand defines the elements of the literary system not as communications but as literary actions, carried by the four roles of producers, mediators (publishers, the book trade), readers and critics.

Schmidt's book is at present the most ambitious attempt to investigate the genesis of modern literature in system-theoretical terms. Whereas Bürger speaks of the literary institution as framing the individual text, Schmidt sees the doctrine of autonomy as the self-descriptive correlate of a self-organising and self-regulating literary system, which differentiates itself in relation to society as a whole and its constituent social systems by means of a process of 'literarisation', that is, the process of the *fictionalisation* of literature in the course of the eighteenth century. By 'fictionalisation' Schmidt means that literature abandons it traditional (premodern) claims to historical or philosophical truth, religious or moral betterment in order to differentiate its own particular 'fictional' form of observing society. The abandonment of the claim to extra-literary truth is at the same time an effective method of immunising the literary system from extra-literary (political or religious) demands and expectations. Literature as fiction gains the freedom to say what it likes. That is to say, it differentiates itself as a system that operates according to its own criteria, just as it emancipates itself from the constraints of patronage through the development of a self-regulating book-market that mediates between production and reception. The growth of literacy and of the reading public in the eighteenth century goes hand in hand not only with an expanding book-production but also with a significant shift in demand. Whereas literary works comprised only a very small proportion of book-production in Germany in the early years of the century, it had increased to over 25 per cent by the end of the century. This demand indicates a need which no other social system could fulfil. What is this social need? Schmidt argues that just as functional differentiation is the evolutionary response to the increasing complexity of society, so the emerging literary system responds to the need for personal orientation in a time of rapid social change. The social function of the literary system can thus be understood as providing in the mode of fiction the classic form for the organisation of individual experience in bourgeois society. This, we may note, is close to what Jauss and Iser propose as literature's social function: the imaginative testing of experience.

The differentiation of literature as a specific form of communication—no longer tied to its traditional function of imitating nature, and thus released from its dependence on received models of reality—opens up a potentially unlimited space for the expression of subjective experience. The literary system 'takes over the communicative exploration of the dimension of subjective learning processes, the multiplication of imaginative models of reality and the innovative anticipation of the possibilities of experience and action in utopias and critiques and offers—at least in theory—the possibility of reconnecting everyday life and culture' (Schmidt, 1989:21, my translation). This makes the literary system the medium of the discovery of the self in the eighteenth century, the site for the unfolding of a self-realising subjectivity. In other words, the self-determining bourgeois subject goes hand in hand with a self-determining literary system; for both, the key word is autonomy, as reflected in the thematisation of the creative freedom of the genius. Literature functions as the medium of this subjective freedom, whose outcome is the pluralisation of interpretations of the world, in which both production and reception are individualised.

Although Schmidt confines himself to the genesis of literature as a social system, he argues in conclusion that there is a basic continuity between the eighteenth century and the present literary system. Here we can see both parallels and differences to Bürger's analysis of the bourgeois institution of literature. Bürger interprets this continuity as the permanent suspension of the emancipatory function of literature in bourgeois society, punctuated only by the failed challenge of the avant-garde movements to the institution. Although Schmidt admits a certain compensatory function for literature, he sees continuity as lying rather in the dynamics of a self-organising system, which resists external interventions and is characterised (like all functionally differentiated systems) by the pressure to innovate, whose outcome is a pluralism of competing programmes and styles. This pluralism means that it is not possible to assign a concretely defined function to the literary system, as can be demonstrated negatively by all attempts to reclaim literature for political or religious or moral purposes. In other words, differentiation can be reversed only at the price of the destruction of the literary system. It is precisely literature's difference from politics or religion or 'life' which constitutes its specificity.

The specificity of modern literature is directly related to the transformation of a premodern social order (based upon hierarchical stratification) into the modern social order, which is based upon the functional differentiation of specialised sub-systems, such as politics, economy, the law, and education. Functional differentiation signals the end of the possibility of grasping society as a whole, as compared with the unity guaranteed by the political and religious hierarchy of stratified society. With the loss of unity there disappears the possibility of a central ordering perspective. It is replaced by the partial perspectives of specialised systems, which compensate for their partial view by means of what Luhmann calls second-order observation. This leads Schwanitz to pose the question of literary evolution in terms of the mode of observation of society. Why was drama supplanted by the novel as the leading genre in the course of the eighteenth century? Schwanitz's answer is that the great period of European drama from Shakespeare to Racine is implicated in the concentration of state power in the monarch, which made the court the centre of political intrigues. The political drama of the court concentrates in itself the fate of society. In other words, the struggles around the throne are already in themselves the drama of power which calls forth its dramatic double. Since the form of drama is direct interaction, the precondition of the rise of European drama was a hierarchically organised society, in which the interactions of the ruling stratum represent society as a whole. The monarch's court is the model of society, and the theatre is the model of the court. In this process of representation, the drama also discovers the difference between observed and observer. Just as the play presents itself as the mirror of the world, as world theatre, so the play-within-the-play (as in *Hamlet* or *A Midsummer Night's Dream*) reveals the representation of the world as a re-presentation. The difference between observer and observed, between the form and the content of the play, can itself be presented on stage. This simultaneous breaking and deepening of the theatrical illusion remains without consequences for the drama only as long as interaction remains the dominant form of the representation of society. This is not the case with modern society, however, where the functionally specialised sphere of politics no longer represents society as whole, and where the media's personalising of politics can be thought of as a vain attempt to conserve the appearance of the drama of politics against the realities of the impersonal bureaucratic complexities of administration. Interaction, however, has moved from the public stage to the private sphere of personal relations. Love, marriage and the family led in the nineteenth century to the drama of conflict between the sexes (Ibsen, Strindberg, Shaw) but in the twentieth century, Schwanitz argues, the representation of private interaction represents nothing but the absence of the public sphere (i.e. the absence of society). The logical conclusion of the disappearance of society from the stage appears in the theatre of the absurd or in Beckett's plays. Drama represents nothing but itself: its subject matter is the impossibility of drama.

The socio-cultural evolution, which has marginalised the dramatic form of interaction as a model of society, has by contrast favoured the rise of the novel as the prime genre for the literary observation of society. Drama, as we have seen, presupposes the visibility of society and presents itself as the microcosm of the social macrocosm. This means that the self-reflection of the dramatic form—the play-within-the-play—can demonstrate the difference between the theatre and the world while yet confirming that all the world's a stage. The novel by contrast replaces the presence of dramatic interaction with the distancing effect of the printed word, just as the collective audience of the drama is replaced by the individual reader. Correspondingly the social microcosm of the drama gives way to the individual perspective of the novelist on society, viewed not in terms of its historical and political unity but as the contemporary setting for private and personal fortunes and misfortunes. The novel thus responds to the separation between political and civil (economic) society, recognised and thematised in the eighteenth century, and analysed by Schmidt as the condition for the emergence of literature as an autonomous literary system. Schwanitz's focus here is the outline of a theory of narrative, which accounts for the difference between the corpus of stories (legends, fables, novellas) that are typical of premodern societies, and the narratives of modern society in the process of rapid change. Schwanitz' starting point accordingly is Cervantes' *Don Quixote* (1605–15), where a new form of the novel emerges precisely out of the contrast between late medieval romances of chivalry and the everyday world of prosaic reality. Appropriately, the first hero of the novel appears as a reader who must discover the difference between old stories and present reality. That is to say (and this is decisive for the new genre), *Don Quixote* distinguishes between fiction and reality in the fiction itself, and this means that the novel has gained the freedom to refer either to itself or to the world—to distinguish in system-theoretical terms between self-reference and external reference. In other words, the novel can observe itself observing the world, and draw the reader's attention to the difference between *what* is narrated and *how* it is narrated. Once this distinction can be drawn, literature can no longer define itself as the imitation of nature, and no longer suppose (as in the case of early modern drama) an essential homology between theatre and world. Modern literature, and typically the novel, compensates (like all other functionally differentiated spheres of communication) for its partial view of society by means of second-order or self-referential observation. Thus the whole repertoire of narrative devices, which register the perspectivism of observation, provide the practice for which the concept of second-order observation offers the theory. It is not by chance that the theory and practice of romantic irony around 1800 closely parallels Luhmann's elaboration of the paradoxes of observation (Roberts, 1992:82ff.), or that a literary scholar has recently suggested that Luhmann uses paradox as the medium for 'humorising' the study of society. Humour functions as an alternative form of hermeneutic understanding, predicated not on the fusion of horizons but on the consciousness of difference. Theoretical humour, in short, is the appropriate mode of responding to the limits of all attempts to reduce the contingency and complexity of the world (Helmstetter, 1993).

Second-order observation involves a change of levels from the *content* to the *form* of observation. The progressive activation of the novel-reader since the eighteenth century, traced by Iser, is clearly related to this change and doubling of levels. The frustration of interpretation, intended by modern literature, has the function of directing attention from what is observed to how it is observed. Fictional narrative becomes conscious of its own procedures, and elaborates complex techniques of observation based on the difference between form and content, that is, between self-reference and external reference. From this difference springs the two main lines of the novel. If novelists orient themselves to the world (external reference), then we have the 'realistic' novel; if they orient themselves to the fictional form, then novelistic self-reflection foregrounds the difference between fiction and reality within the fiction. The self-referential novel makes explicit what remains implicit in the realistic novel—the difference between first- and second-order observation. In this sense we can agree with Iser that the reader of the realistic novel is an 'implicit' reader, whose task is the testing of experience, the discovery of differences between the manifest and latent motivation of the characters. The self-referential novel by contrast observes itself observing the world, and discovers thereby the latency or unconscious of its own form. If the realistic novel is directed to exploring the conditions of the possibility of experience, the self-referential novel is directed to exploring the conditions of the possibility of narration, and it is for this reason that it explicitly thematises the function of the reader.

Second-order observation could be seen as offering a common point of reference not only for Iser and Jauss's reader-reception theory (hermeneutics) but also for Bürger's theory of the literary institution (critical literary theory). Whether the focus is the reader's concretisation of the text, or the norms governing reception, in each case we are dealing with second-order accounts, which involve a circular relation between cause and effect. Thus for Iser the reader constructs and is constructed by the text. Similarly Bürger writes: 'The institution functions within the work, just as the work functions within the institution'. The paradox of circular causality is central to the idea of self-organisation, which comes into ever sharper focus as we move from the hermeneutics of the text to the institution of literature, and to the conception of literature as a functionally differentiated social system.

The idea of circular causality is central to the systems-theoretical understanding of autonomy as the process by which a system separates itself from its environment and uses this difference for its own operations. The advantage of this approach is that it offers a new way of tackling two perennial problems of literary theory: the relation between literature and society, and the relation between literature and reality. As we have seen, the relation between literature (the literary series) and 'general history' is transformed by reception theory into the project of a history of the reception of literary works, and by Peter Bürger into an enquiry into the ideological determinants of reception. Systems theory reformulates this question in terms of social evolution. The constitution of a separate social system for literature is part of the history of the functional differentiation of society: the autonomy of the literary system is one with the autonomy of differentiated society as a whole. This allows us to distinguish between the doctrine of autonomy, which Bürger sees as defining the social function of literature since the end of the eighteenth century, and the autonomy of the literary system. The doctrine of autonomy then appears as one—even if perhaps the most important—of many competing programmes and self-descriptions of the literary system. Secondly, instead of asking how works of literature reflect or represent an external reality, systems theory reverses the question of 'realism' by asking how the literary system uses, for the purpose of observation, the difference from its environment. And here we can see how second-order observation corresponds to what Habermas calls 'decentred consciousness', that is, our ability as moderns to adopt a hypothetical attitude to the world. This is true not only of the scientific attitude but also of literature's imaginative testing of experience. The fictionalisation of literature signifies the emergence of a specific experimental observation of the world, which can no longer be understood as the representation of a 'real' world independent of the observer.

Bibliography

1 Introduction

David Roberts

Adorno, Theodor W. et al. (eds) (1976) *The Positivist Dispute in German Sociology*, London: Heinemann [1969]

Bubner, Rüdiger (1981) *Modern German Philosophy*, trans. Eric Williams, Cambridge: Cambridge University Press

Gadamer, Hans-Georg (1989) *Truth and Method*, 2nd rev. edn, trans. G. Barden and J. Cumming, London: Sheed and Ward [1960]

Habermas, Jürgen (1988) *On the Logic of the Social Sciences*, trans. S. Nicholsen and J. Stark, Cambridge, Massachusetts: MIT Press [1970]

Luhmann, Niklas (1987) 'Modern System Theory and the Theory of Society' in Volker Meja et al. (eds), *Modern German Sociology*, New York: Columbia University Press, pp. 173–86

—— (1990) 'Complexity and Meaning' in Niklas Luhmann, *Essays in Self-Reference*, New York: Columbia University Press, pp. 80–5

2 Gadamer and the Circles of Hermeneutics

John Rundell

Bauman, Zygmunt (1978) *Hermeneutics and Social Science*, London: Hutchinson

Bernstein, Richard (1982) 'From Hermeneutics to Praxis', *Review of Metaphysics*, 35, pp. 823–45

—— (1985) *Beyond Objectivism and Relativism*, Oxford: Basil Blackwell

Bruns, Gerald L. (1992) *Hermeneutics: Ancient and Modern*, New Haven, Connecticut: Yale University Press

Bubner, Rüdiger (1981) *Modern German Philosophy*, trans. Eric Williams, Cambridge: Cambridge University Press

Connolly, J. M. and Keutner, Th. (eds) (1988) *Hermeneutics versus Science? Three German Views*, Notre Dame, Indiana: University of Notre Dame Press

DiCenso, James (1990) *Hermeneutics and the Disclosure of Truth*, Charlottesville: University Press of Virginia

Dilthey, Wilhelm (1976) *Selected Writings*, ed., trans. and intro. H. P. Richman, Cambridge: Cambridge University Press

—— (1990) 'The Rise of Hermeneutics' in Ormiston and Schrift (eds), *The Hermeneutic Tradition From Ast to Ricoeur*, pp. 101–14

Ermath, Michael (1981) 'The Transformation of Hermeneutics: Nineteenth Century Ancients and Twentieth Century Moderns', *Monist*, 64, 2, pp. 175–94

Feher, Ferenc (1991) 'Between Relativism and Fundamentalism: Hermeneutic as Europe's Mainstream Political Tradition' in A. Heller and F. Feher (eds) *The Grandeur and Twilight of Radical Universalism*, New Brunswick, New Jersey: Transaction Publishers, pp. 551–68 [First published 1989 as 'Hermeneutic as Europe's Mainstream Political Tradition', *Thesis Eleven* 22, pp. 79–91]

Frank, Manfred (1989) *What is Neo-Structuralism?*, trans. Sabine Wilke and Richard Gray, Minneapolis: University of Minnesota Press [Ger 1984]

Frisby, David (1976) *The Positivist Dispute in German Sociology*, London: Heinemann

Gadamer, Hans-Georg (1977) *Philosophical Hermeneutics*, trans. and ed. by David E. Linge, Berkeley: University of California Press

—— (1979) 'The Problem of Historical Consciousness' in Rabinow and Sullivan (eds) *Interpretive Social Science*, pp. 82–140

—— (1981) *Reason in the Age of Science*, trans. Frederick G. Lawrence, Cambridge, Massachusetts: MIT Press

—— (1986) 'Text and Interpretation' in Wachterhauser (ed.) *Hermeneutics and Modern Philosophy*, pp. 377–96

—— (1989) *Truth and Method*, 2nd rev. edn, trans. and revised by Joel Weinsheimer and Donald G. Marshall, London: Sheed and Ward [Ger 1960]

—— (1990) 'A Reply to my Critics', in Ormiston and Schrift (eds) *The Hermeneutic Tradition From Ast to Ricoeur*, pp. 273–97

Giddens, Anthony (1984) *The Constitution of Society*, Cambridge: Polity Press

Habermas, Jürgen (1988) *On the Logic of the Social Sciences*, trans. Shierry Weber Nicholsen and Jerry A. Stark, Cambridge, Massachusetts: MIT Press [Ger 1967]

—— (1990a) 'A review of Gadamer's *Truth and Method*' in Ormiston and Schrift (eds) *The Hermeneutic Tradition From Ast to Ricoeur*, pp. 213–44

—— (1990b) 'The Hermeneutic Claim to Universality' in Ormiston and Schrift (eds) *The Hermeneutic Tradition From Ast to Ricoeur*, pp. 245–72

—— (1990c) 'Reconstruction and Interpretation in the Human Sciences' in Jürgen Habermas, *Moral Consciousness and Communicative Action*, trans. Christian Lenhardt and Shierry Weber Nicholsen, intro. Thomas McCarthy, Cambridge, Massachusetts: MIT Press [1983]

—— (1992) *Postmetaphysical Thinking: Philosophical Essays*, trans. William Mark Hohengarten, Cambridge, Massachusetts: MIT Press

Hegel, Georg (1979) *Phenomenology of Spirit*, trans. A. V. Miller, Oxford: Oxford University Press [Ger 1807]

Heidegger, Martin (1973) 'Letter On Humanism' in R. M. Zaner and D. Ihde, *Phenomenology and Existentialism*, New York: Capricorn Books [1947]

—— (1985) *Being and Time*, trans. John Macquarie and Edward Robinson, Oxford: Basil Blackwell [Ger 1927]

—— (1993) *Basic Writings*, ed. David Farnell Krell, London: Routledge

—— (1993) 'Origin of the Work of Art' in *Basic Writings* [Ger 1936]

—— (1993) 'What is Called Thinking?' in *Basic Writings* [Ger 1954]

Heller, Agnes (1988) 'Europe an Epilogue?' in A. Heller and F. Feher (eds) *The Postmodern Political Condition*, Cambridge: Polity Press, pp. 146–60

Kant, Immanuel (1978) *Critique of Pure Reason*, trans. Norman Kemp Smith, London: Macmillan [Ger 1781]

Kelly, Michael (1990) 'MacIntyre, Habermas and Philosophical Ethics' in Michael Kelly (ed.) *Hermeneutics and Critical Theory*, Cambridge, Massachusetts: MIT Press

MacIntyre, Alasdair (1985) *After Virtue*, 2nd edn, London: Duckworth

Mendelson, Jack (1979) 'The Habermas–Gadamer Debate', *New German Critique* 18, pp. 44–71

Michelfelder, D. P. and R. E. Palmer (1989) *Dialogue and Deconstruction The Gadamer–Derrida Encounter*, Albany: State University of New York Press

Misgeld, Dieter (1977) 'Critical Theory and Hermeneutics: The Debate between Habermas and Gadamer' in J. O'Neill (ed.) *On Critical Theory*, London: Heinemann

—— (1981) 'Science, Hermeneutics, and the Utopian Content of the "Liberal-Democratic Tradition". On Habermas's Recent Work: A Reply to Habermas', *New German Critique* 22, pp. 123–44

Mueller-Vollmer, Kurt (1986a) 'Introduction: Language, Mind and Artefact: An Outline of Hermeneutic Theory Since the Enlightenment' in Mueller-Vollmer (ed.) *The Hermeneutics Reader*, pp. 2–53

—— (1986b) *The Hermeneutics Reader*, Oxford: Basil Blackwell

Ormiston, G. L. and A. D. Schrift (1990a) *The Hermeneutic Tradition From Ast to Ricoeur*, Albany: State University of New York Press

—— (1990b) *Transforming the Hermeneutic Context From Nietzsche to Nancy*, Albany: State University of New York Press

Palmer, Richard (1969) *Hermeneutics: Interpretation Theory in Schleiermacher, Dilthey, Heidegger and Gadamer*, Evanston, Illinois: Northwestern University Press

Plato (1989) *The Collected Dialogues*, ed. Edith Hamilton and Huntington Cairns, Princeton, New Jersey: Princeton University Press

Rabinow, P. and W. M. Sullivan (eds) (1979) *Interpretive Social Science. A Second Look* Berkeley: University of California Press

Schleiermacher, F. D. E. (1977) *Hermeneutics: The Handwritten Manuscripts*, ed. Heinz Kimmerle, trans. J. Duke and J. Fostman, Georgia: Scholars Press

Schnädelbach, H. (1984) *Philosophy in Germany: 1831–1933* Cambridge: Cambridge University Press

Shalin, Dimitri (1986) 'Romanticism and the Rise of Sociological Hermeneutics', *Social Research* 53, pp. 77–123

Shapiro, G. and A. D. Sica (1984) *Hermeneutics: Questions and Prospects*, Amhurst: University of Massachusetts Press

Silverman, H. G. and Don Ihde (1985) *Hermeneutics and Deconstruction*, Albany: State University of New York Press

Taylor, Charles (1971) 'Interpretation and the Sciences of Man', *Review of Metaphysics* 25, pp. 3–51

—— (1975) *Hegel*, Cambridge: Cambridge University Press

—— (1980) 'Understanding in Social Science', *Review of Metaphysics* 34, pp. 3–23

Wachterhauser, B. P. (1986) *Hermeneutics and Modern Philosophy*, Albany: State University of New York Press

Wright, Kathleen (1990) *Festivals of Interpretation. Essays on Hans-Georg Gadamer's Work*, Albany: State University of New York Press

3 Critical Theory—Jürgen Habermas

Peter Beilharz

Abendroth, W. (1972) *A Short History of the European Working Class*, London: New Left Books

Adorno, T. W. (1974) *Minima Moralia*, London: New Left Books [1951]

Arato, A. and J. Cohen (1992) *Civil Society and Political Theory*, Cambridge, Massachusetts: MIT Press

Arato, A. and E. Gebhardt (eds) (1978) *The Essential Frankfurt School Reader*, Oxford: Blackwell

Beilharz, P. (ed.) (1992) *Social Theory—A Guide to Central Thinkers*, Sydney: Allen and Unwin

—— (1994) *Postmodern Socialism*, Carlton: Melbourne University Press

Benjamin, W. (1968) *Illuminations*, New York: Schocken [1940]

Bernstein, R. (ed.) (1985) *Habermas and Modernity*, Oxford: Polity Press

Brand, A. (1989) *The Force of Reason: An Introduction to Habermas*, Sydney: Allen and Unwin

Calhoun, C. (ed.) (1992) *Habermas and the Public Sphere*, Cambridge, Massachusetts: MIT Press

Callinicos, A. (1989) *Against Postmodernism*, Oxford: Polity Press

Dews, P. (ed.) (1992) *Autonomy and Solidarity: Interviews with Jürgen Habermas*, London: Verso

Dubiel, H. (1985) *Theory and Politics*, Cambridge, Massachusetts: MIT Press

—— (1992) 'Domination or Emancipation? The Debate over the Heritage of Critical Theory' in Honneth et al. (eds) *Cultural-Political Interventions in the Unfinished Project of Enlightenment*, pp. 3–16

Forester, J. (1985) *Critical Theory and Public Life*, Cambridge, Massachusetts: MIT Press

Gadamer, H. (1975) *Truth and Method*, New York: Seabury

Gilligan, C. (1982) *In a Different Voice*, Cambridge, Massachusetts: Harvard University Press

Habermas, J. (1970) *Toward a Rational Society*, trans. J. Schapiro, Boston: Beacon [Ger 1968–69]

—— (1971) *Knowledge and Human Interests*, trans. J. Schapiro, Boston: Beacon [Ger 1968]

—— (1973) *Theory and Practice*, trans. J. Viertel, Boston: Beacon [Ger 1968]

—— (1975) *Legitimation Crisis*, trans. T. McCarthy, Boston: Beacon [Ger 1973]

—— (1979) *Communication and the Evolution of Society*, trans. T. McCarthy, Boston: Beacon [Ger 1976]

—— (1981) 'Modernity versus Postmodernity', *New German Critique* 22, pp. 3–14

—— (1983) *Philosophical-Political Profiles*, trans. F. Lawrence, Cambridge, Massachusetts: MIT Press [Ger 1971/1973]

—— (1984) *Observations on 'The Spiritual Situation of the Age'*, Cambridge, Massachusetts: MIT Press

—— (1984, 1987) *Theory of Communicative Action*, trans. T. McCarthy, Boston: Beacon [Ger 1981]

—— (1987) *The Philosophical Discourse of Modernity*, trans. F. Lawrence, Boston: Beacon [Ger 1985]

—— (1988) *On the Logic of the Social Sciences*, trans. S. Nicholsen and J. Stark, Cambridge, Massachusetts: MIT Press [Ger 1967]

—— (1989) *The Structural Transformation of the Public Sphere*, trans. T. Burger, Cambridge, Massachusetts: MIT Press [Ger 1962]

____ (1989b) *The New Conservatism: Cultural Criticism and the Historians' Debate*, Cambridge, Massachusetts: MIT Press

—— (1990) *Moral Consciousness and Communicative Action*, trans. F. Lawrence, Boston, Beacon [Ger 1983]

—— (1992) *Post-Metaphysical Thinking*, Cambridge, Massachusetts: MIT Press

—— (1993) *Justification and Application*, Cambridge, Massachusetts: MIT Press

Held, D. (1980) *Introduction to Critical Theory: Horkheimer to Habermas*, London: Heinemann

Holub, R. C. (1991) *Jürgen Habermas: Critic in the Public Sphere*, London: Routledge

Honneth, A. (1991) *Critique of Power: Reflective Stages in a Critical Social Theory*, Cambridge, Massachusetts: MIT Press

Honneth, A. and H. Joas (eds) (1991) *Communicative Action*, Oxford: Polity Press

Honneth, A. et al. (eds) (1992a) *Cultural-Political Interventions in the Unfinished Project of Enlightenment*, Cambridge, Massachusetts: MIT Press

Honneth, A. et al. (eds) (1992b) *Philosophical Interventions in the Unfinished Project of Enlightenment*, Cambridge, Massachusetts: MIT Press

Horkheimer, M. (1972) *Critical Theory: Selected Essays*, New York: Continuum

Horkheimer, M. and T. W. Adorno (1973) *Dialectic of Enlightenment*, trans. J. Cuming, London: Allen Lane [Ger 1947]

Jay, M. (1973) *The Dialectical Imagination*, Boston: Little Brown

Keane, J. (1988) *Democracy and Civil Society*, London: Verso

Löwith, K. (1982) *Max Weber and Karl Marx*, London: Allen and Unwin [1932]

Lukács, G. (1971) *History and Class Consciousness*, London: Merlin [1923]

Lyotard, J. F. (1984) *The Postmodern Condition*, Minneapolis: University of Minnesota Press

McCarthy, T. (1984) *The Critical Theory of Jürgen Habermas*, Cambridge, Massachusetts: MIT Press

Marcuse, H. (1964) *One Dimensional Man*, London: Sphere

Meja, V. et al. (eds) (1987) *Modern German Sociology*, New York: Columbia University Press

Negt, O. and A. Kluge (1993) *Public Sphere and Experience*, trans. P. Labany, Minneapolis: University of Minnesota Press [1972]

Parsons, T. (1937) *The Structure of Social Action*, New York: Free Press

—— (1951) *The Social System*, New York: Free Press

Peukert, H. (1989) *Science, Action and Fundamental Theology: Toward a Theology of Communicative Action*, Cambridge, Massachusetts: MIT Press

Pusey, M. (1987) *Jürgen Habermas*, London: Ellis Horwood

Rasmussen, D. (1990) *Reading Habermas*, Oxford: Blackwell

Roderick, R. (1985) *Habermas and the Foundations of Critical Theory*, London: Macmillan

Seidman, S. (ed.) (1989) *Jürgen Habermas on Society and Politics: A Reader*, Boston: Beacon

Thompson, J. and D. Held (eds) (1982) *Habermas: Critical Debates*, London: Macmillan

Touraine, A. (1987) *Return of the Actor: Social Theory in Post-industrial Society*, Minneapolis: University of Minnesota Press

White, S. (1988) *The Recent Work of Jürgen Habermas*, London: Macmillan

4 Niklas Luhmann and the Theory of Social Systems

Paul R. Harrison

Beck, Ulrich (1992) *Risk Society: Towards a New Modernity*, London: Sage [1986]

Brown, George Spencer (1969) *Laws of Form*, London: Allen and Unwin

Giddens, Anthony (1984) *The Constitution of Society: Outline of the Theory of Structuration*, Cambridge: Polity Press

Habermas, Jürgen (1971) *Knowledge and Human Interests*, trans. J. Shapiro, Boston: Beacon [1968]

—— (1987) *The Philosophical Discourse of Modernity*, trans. F. Lawrence, Boston: Beacon [1985]

Habermas, Jürgen and Niklas Luhmann (1971) *Theorie der Gesellschaft oder Sozialtechnologie—Was leistet die Systemforschung? Theorie-Diskussion*, Frankfurt am Main: Suhrkamp

Luhmann, Niklas (1973) *Zweckbegriff und Systemrationalität: Über die Funktion von Zwecken in Sozialen Systemen*, Frankfurt am Main: Suhrkamp

—— (1979) *Trust and Power: Two Works by Niklas Luhmann*, trans. H. Davis, J. Raffan and K. Rooney, Chichester: Wiley [1973, 1975]

—— (1980) *Gesellschaftstruktur und Semantik: Semantik zur Wissenssoziologie der modernen Gesellschaft, Band 1*. Frankfurt am Main: Suhrkamp

—— (1982) *The Differentiation of Society*, trans. S. Holmes and C. Larmore, New York: Columbia University Press

—— (1985a) *Soziale Systeme: Grundriß einer Allgemeinen Theorie*, 2nd edn, Frankfurt am Main: Suhrkamp

—— (1985b) *A Sociological Theory of Law*, trans. E. King and M. Albrow, London: Routledge and Kegan Paul [1981]

—— (1986) *Love as Passion: The Codification of Intimacy*, trans. J. Gaines and D. Jones, Cambridge: Polity [1982]

—— (1987) 'Die Richtigkeit Soziologischer Theorie', *Merkur* 455, January, pp. 36–49

—— (1989) *Ecological Communication*, trans. J. Bednarz, London: Polity [1986]

—— (1990a) *Essays on Self-Reference*, New York: Columbia University Press

—— (1990b) *Die Wissenschaft der Gesellschaft*, Frankfurt am Main: Suhrkamp

—— (1990c) *Soziologische Aufklärung: Konstruktivistische Perspektiven*, Opladen: Westdeutscher Verlag

—— (1990d) *Political Theory in the Welfare State*, trans. J. Bednarz, Berlin: Walter de Gruyter [1981]

—— (1991) *Soziologie des Risikos*, Berlin: Walter de Gruyter

—— (1992a) 'The concept of society', *Thesis Eleven* 31, pp. 67–80

—— (1992b) *Beobachtungen der Moderne*, Opladen: Westdeutscher Verlag

—— (1993) 'Deconstruction as Second-order Observing', *New Literary History* 24, pp. 763–82

McCarthy, Thomas (1984) *The Critical Theory of Jürgen Habermas*, Cambridge, Massachusetts: MIT Press

Mann, Michael (1986) *The Sources of Social Power: A History of Power from the Beginning to AD 1760*, Cambridge: Cambridge University Press

Maturana, Umberto R. and Francisco J. Varela (1980) *Autopoiesis and Cognition: The Realization of the Living*, Dordrecht: Boston

von Foerster, Heinz (1963) *Observing Systems*, Seaside, California: Intersystems

5 From Text to System: Recent German Literary Theory

David Roberts

Adorno, Theodor W. (1984) *Aesthetic Theory*, trans. C. Lenhardt, London: Routledge [1970]

—— (1991, 1992) *Notes to Literature*, trans. S. Nicholsen, 2 vols, New York: Columbia University Press

Bürger, Peter (1984) *The Theory of the Avant-Garde*, trans. M. Shaw, Minneapolis: University of Minnesota Press [1974]

—— (1985a) 'Literary Institution and Modernization', *Poetics* 14, pp. 419–33

—— (1985b) 'On Literary History', *Poetics* 14, pp. 199–207

—— (1990) 'The Problem of Aesthetic Value' in Peter Collier and Helga Geyer-Ryan (eds) *Literary Theory Today*, Cambridge: Polity Press, pp. 22–34

—— (1992) *The Decline of Modernism*, trans. N. Walker, Cambridge: Polity Press

Bürger, Peter and Christa Bürger (1992) *The Institutions of Art*, trans. L. Kruger, Introduction by Russell A. Berman, Lincoln: University of Nebraska Press

Fish, Stanley (1980) *Is There a Text in this Class? The Authority of Interpretive Communities*, Cambridge, Massachusetts: Harvard University Press

Freund, Elizabeth (1987) *The Return of the Reader: Reader-Response Criticism*, London: Methuen

Gadamer, Hans-Georg (1975) *Truth and Method*, 2nd rev. edn, London: Sheed and Ward [1960]

Habermas, Jürgen (1987) *The Philosophical Discourse of Modernity*, trans. F. Lawrence, Cambridge: Polity Press

—— (1988) *On the Logic of the Social Sciences*, trans. S. Nicholsen and J. Stark, Cambridge, Massachusetts: MIT Press

Helmstetter, Rudolf (1993) 'Die weißen Mäuse des Sinns; Luhmanns Humorisierung der Wissenschaft der Gesellschaft', *Merkur* July, pp. 601–19

Hohendahl, Peter Uwe (1991) *Reappraisals: Shifting Alignments in Postwar Critical Theory*, Ithaca, New York: Cornell University Press

Holub, Robert (1984) *Reception Theory: A Critical Introduction*, London: Methuen

Iser, Wolfgang (1974) *The Implied Reader: Patterns of Communication in Prose Fiction from Bunyan to Beckett*, Baltimore, Maryland: Johns Hopkins University Press

—— (1978) *The Act of Reading: A Theory of Aesthetic Response*, Baltimore, Maryland: Johns Hopkins University Press [1976]

—— (1989) *Prospecting: From Reader Response to Literary Anthropology*, Baltimore, Maryland: Johns Hopkins University Press

Jauss, Hans Robert (1982a) *Aesthetic Experience and Literary Hermeneutics*, trans. M. Shaw, Minneapolis: University of Minnesota Press

—— (1982b) *Toward an Aesthetic of Reception*, trans. T. Bahti, Minneapolis: University of Minnesota Press

—— (1989) *Question and Answer: Forms of Dialogic Understanding*, ed. and trans. with a foreword by Michael Hays, Minneapolis: University of Minnesota Press

Luhmann, Niklas (1985) 'The Work of Art and the Self-Reproduction of Art', *Thesis Eleven* 12, pp. 4–27

—— (1987) 'The Medium of Art', *Thesis Eleven* 18–19, pp. 101–13

—— (1993) 'Deconstruction as Second-order Observing', *New Literary History* 24, pp. 763–82

Marcuse, Herbert (1968) 'The Affirmative Character of Culture' in Herbert Marcuse *Negations: Essays in Critical Theory*, Boston: Beacon

—— (1969) *Essay on Liberation*, London: Allen Lane

Roberts, David (1992) 'The Paradox of Form: Literature and Self-reference', *Poetics* 21, pp. 75–91

Schmidt, Siegfried J. (1980) 'Fictionality in Literary and Non-Literary Discourse', *Poetics* 9, pp. 525–46

—— (1983) 'On the Concept of System and its Use in Literary Studies', *Poetics* 12, pp. 19–34

—— (1989) *Die Selbstorganisation des Sozialsystems Literatur im 18. Jahrhundert*, Frankfurt am Main: Suhrkamp

—— (1991a) 'From Literary Discourses to the Social System of Literature', *Thesis Eleven* 29, pp. 95–104 [translation of chapter 1, Schmidt (1989)]

—— (1991b) 'Text Understanding—A Self-Organizing Cognitive Process', *Poetics* 20, pp. 273–301

—— (1991c) 'Literary Systems as Self-Organizing Systems' in E. Ibsch, D. Schram and G. Steen (eds) *Empirical Studies of Literature*, Amsterdam: Rodolphi, pp. 177–83

Schwanitz, Dietrich (1987) 'Systems Theory and the Environment of Theory' in C. Koelb and V. Lokke (eds) *The Current in Criticism: Essays on the Present and Future of Literary Theory*, West Lafayette: Purdue University Press, pp. 265–94

—— (1990) *Systemtheorie und Literatur: Ein neues Paradigma*, Opladen: Westdeutscher Verlag

Wellmer, Albrecht (1991) *The Persistence of Modernism: Essays on Aesthetics, Ethics and Postmodernism*, trans. D. Midgley, Cambridge: Polity Press

Index

Compiled by Lee White

Durkheim, Emile, 51, 67; and social
differentiation theory, 73

ecological movement, 67
Elias, Norbert, 2
Enlightenment, 1, 13, 16, 18, 87, 88,
97; and Habermas, 3, 57; and literature, 104; and Luhmann, 3; and
outrage, 54; and Romanticism, 15;
concept of art, 105; Gadamer's
critique of, 30–1
environment, Luhmann's view, 72
environmentally-open systems theory,
69, 71
epistemological hermeneutics, 19
equilibrium theories, 69
Essay on Liberation, 102
evolution: and globalisation, 83; and
risk, 81–2; literary, 94; Luhmann's
view, 76, 86
evolutionism: and functionalism, 85;
Giddens's views, 86; Luhmann's
views, 74–5, 86; Mann's views,
85–6; versus anti-evolutionism, 67
'expressivist turn', 18

fiction: and freedom, 108, 109; and
observation, 112, 113, 114; and
organisation of individual, 109; as
horizon of world, 99; function of,
97–8; literary evolution of, 111–
12
'fore-structure', 23, 30
Formalist, approach to literary production, 93, 94
Foucault, Michel, 1, 26, 40, 41, 51,
53, 58; Habermas's view, 55, 60,
61; Luhmann's view, 76
Frankfurt School, 1, 2, 26, 39, 40,
47, 52, 62, 91; and Marxism, 62–3
Freud, Sigmund, 41, 45, 48, 53, 61
Fromm, Erich, 40
functionalism, 1, 6
fusion of horizons, 33, 34, 36, 92,
96; and humour, 112; in reading
process, 98

Gadamer, Hans-Georg, 3, 92; and
Dilthey, 26, 27–8, 29; and Habermas, 35–8, 59, 61; and Heidegger,
20, 24, 25, 26, 27, 32, 34, 35; and
Schleiermacher, 26–7, 28, 29, 32,
33; dispute with Habermas, 35–8;
hermeneutic circles, 10ff., 32, 35,
36; hermeneutics, 4, 103; horizons, 33, 34; intersubjectivity, 19,
28–9; ontology of hermeneutical
reflection, 25ff.; subjectivity, 30;
theory of, 4–5
Gauchet, Marcel, 79
Gehlen, Arnold, 1, 2
Geisteswissenschaften, 11
gender differences, 59, 60
Giddens, Anthony, 13, 41, 67, 84;
on reflexivity, 84
Gilligan, Carol, 47, 59
globalisation, 67; Luhmann's view,
82–4

Habermas, Jürgen, 1, 2, 26, 84, 91,
97, 104, 114; and Enlightenment,
3, 57; and Gadamer, 35–8, 59, 61;
and Foucault, 55, 60, 61; and
Kant, 48; and Kohlberg, 59–60,
61; and Luhmann, 59, 68–9, 87;
and Lyotard, 60–1, 62; and Marx,
50–3 *passim*, 62; and Marxism, 39,
41, 44–5, 46, 47, 49, 54, 62; and
Nazism, 44; and Parsons, 51; and
Weber, 3, 50, 51; comparisons
between Gadamer and Luhmann,
4–5, 6–7; Critical Theory of, 39ff.,
50–1, 63–4; critique of Heidegger,
55; democracy, 3; English trans-
lations of, 42–3; French tradition,
53–4; functionalism, 4; hermeneutics, 59; modernity, 41, 44, 51,
53, 54, 57, 58; moral development,
59; rationality, 50; reception process, 41–2; textual argument, 52;
theory of, 5–6, 53, 54
Habermas and the Public Sphere, 58
Hegel, Georg, 9, 31, 32, 97
Heidegger, Martin, 1, 2, 19, 32, 92,
97; Habermas's critique, 55; hermeneutic circle, 19–24; interpretation, 23; language, 20, 23, 24,
25; question of Being, 21–2, 24;
untruth, 29
Hempel, Carl, 56

After Mabo

Interpreting indigenous traditions

TIM ROWSE

Many non-Aboriginal Australians, sensitive to the fact that their nation came into existence through the conquest and dispossession of indigenous peoples, continue to seek ways of righting historical wrongs. A significant stage was reached in the High Court's so-called Mabo decision of June 1992, which recognised a 'native right in land'. Tim Rowse draws on history, political science, anthropology, cultural studies, ecology and archaeology to critique non-Aboriginal ways of perceiving Aboriginality. He focuses on the moral and legal traditions of settlers and indigenous peoples, their different attitudes towards the environment, the institutional heritage of 'Aboriginal welfare', tensions between indigenous cultures and indigenous politics, and the representation of Aboriginal identities by Aboriginal writers.

> *'a stylish and shrewd book . . . should be read by all who try to follow Mabo'* Barry Hill, Age

The Architecture of Babel

Discourses of literature and science

DAMIEN BRODERICK

Today the humanities seem painfully severed from the sciences. Writers, artists and ordinary thinking citizens cannot readily understand the sciences that have reshaped modern life. Scientists in turn find critical theory difficult and elusive. Drawing on recent semiotic and post-structural approaches to the text, Damien Broderick provides a critical introduction to recent efforts to construct an interdisciplinary analysis of the 'two cultures', literature and science. He finds literary theorists deficient in scientific rigour, and would like scientists to acquire the linguistic sophistication of humanists and their postmodern successors. Both literary theories and scientific practices, he concludes, are deeply implicated in social contexts.

> *'an intriguing intellectual tour through exciting territory, much of which is at the cutting edge of literary and scientific philosophy'* Robyn Arianrhod, Age

The Body in the Text

ANNE CRANNY-FRANCIS

Male/female, white/black, mind/body: these fundamental distinctions, based on the way we see ourselves and others, face irrevocable breakdown as we stand on the edge of revolutions in artificial intelligence, robotics and genetic engineering. Cranny-Francis gives a lucid and stylish introduction to the ways in which the body is represented in our culture. Her clear, considered analysis shows how these representations are used as critiques of contemporary society by writers on gender, sexuality, race and class, and describes how these representations have changed the relationships between our understandings of the body and the ways in which we live and think about our world.

Debating Derrida

NIALL LUCY

'There is nothing outside the text.' Possibly no single statement has caused such a storm in critical theory as this famous observation by the French philosopher, Jacques Derrida. While it is often misunderstood as meaning that nothing is real, *Debating Derrida* demonstrates that Derrida's philosophy does not lack political conviction.

Niall Lucy examines three key terms–text, writing and *différance*–as they are used in three famous debates: Derrida's disputes over speech-acts with John R. Searle, over discourse with Michel Foucault and over apartheid. Lucy also takes up the issue of Derrida's relationship to postmodernism. *Debating Derrida* decisively shows that instead of disagreeing with Derrida, we should rather be defending him.

A Foucault Primer

Discourse, power and the subject

ALEC McHOUL AND WENDY GRACE

The French historian and philosopher, Michel Foucault, has had a profound influence on scholars in the humanities and social sciences for the last three decades. This book is designed for those attempting to come to grips with Foucault's voluminous and complex writings. Instead of dealing with them chronologically, however, *A Foucault Primer* concentrates on some of their central concepts, primarily Foucault's rethinking of the categories of discourse, power and the subject (or subjectivity).

> '*As an introductory account designed for the non-specialist reader, this book stands out*' Paul Patton, University of Sydney

Literary Formations

Post-colonialism, nationalism, globalism

ANNE BREWSTER

Literary Formations provides a detailed examination of post-colonial literatures and literary theory. Writing from a feminist perspective, Brewster introduces the issue of gender into a field that has been widely dominated by questions of race and nationalism. She investigates the genre of Aboriginal women's autobiography and looks at the contrasting approaches to nationalism of two 'ethnic' women writers–Bharati Mukherjee in the USA and Ania Walwicz in Australia. Scrutinising the processes of neo-colonisation and the ways in which indigenous, diasporic and multicultural writing are reappropriated by the canon, *Literary Formations* is a valuable introduction to this influential area of critical thinking.

Masculinities and Identities

DAVID BUCHBINDER

Why does masculinity find itself in crisis? This book traces some causes, as well as the developing interest in masculinity and the creation of men's studies, from their origins in feminist and gay political activist theory. David Buchbinder examines the dynamics at work in various cultural constructions of masculinity, not all of which meet with approval in a patriarchal culture. The effects on men of patriarchal ideologies, phallocentrism and male sexuality (both heterosexual and homosexual) are among the issues discussed, while different strands of masculine discourse are identified and examined in a variety of texts ranging from opera to recent news stories.

> *'a timely, sensible and sensitive book' David Gilbey,* Australian Book Review

Postmodern Socialism

PETER BEILHARZ

Injustice, poverty, living and working conditions: the attempt to deal with these social questions arose from a nineteenth-century recognition of the complex problems created mainly in cities. At the same time socialism emerged from a romantic stream of Enlightenment concerned with nature and simplicity. Socialist arguments, now widely viewed as discredited, tackled these problems that ironically remain with us in these postmodern times. By juxtaposing postmodernity and socialism we can generate illuminating perspectives on the way we live *now. Postmodern Socialism* traces and criticises these perspectives.

> *'an intellectual* tour de force . . . *a vital contribution to the debate on* la fin de socialisme' *Manfred Steger,* Critical Sociology

Theories of Desire

PATRICK FUERY

Lacan, Barthes, Derrida, Foucault, Kristeva, Cixous, Irigaray: these critical theorists are all linked by their analyses of desire. *Theories of Desire* looks not only at the role of desire in the works of these writers but also examines other major issues and themes of post-structuralism. Fuery considers the place of desire in psychoanalysis, philosophy, literary studies and feminism. He highlights the connections between desire and the critical analysis of subjectivity, language and culture. He investigates the institutionalisation of desire, the relationship between language, discourse and desire, and notes the problems of dealing with women's desire in phallocentric contexts.